I0411478

United States
Department of
Agriculture

Forest Service

**Northeastern
Research Station**

General Technical
Report NE-337

Proceedings
16th U.S. Department of Agriculture Interagency Research Forum on Gypsy Moth and Other Invasive Species, 2005

the sixteenth
usda interagency research forum
on gypsy moth and other invasive species

"untangling
the
knots"

january 18-21, 2005
loews annapolis hotel
annapolis, maryland

The findings and conclusions of each article in this publication are those of
the individual author(s) and do not necessarily represent the views of the U.S.
Department of Agriculture Forest Service. All articles were received in digital format
and were edited for uniform type and style; each author is responsible for the
accuracy and content of his or her own paper.

The use of trade, firm, or corporation names in this publication is for the information
and convenience of the reader. Such use does not constitute an official endorsement
or approval by the U. S. Department of Agriculture or the Forest Service of any
product or service to the exclusion of others that may be suitable.

Remarks about pesticides appear in some technical papers
contained in these proceedings. Publication of these statements
does not constitute endorsement or recommendation of them by
the conference sponsors, nor does it imply that uses discussed
have been registered. Use of most pesticides is regulated by State
and Federal Law. Applicable regulations must be obtained from the
appropriate regulatory agencies.

CAUTION: Pesticides can be injurious to humans, domestic animals, desirable
plants, and fish and other wildlife—if they are not handled and applied properly. Use
all pesticides selectively and carefully. Follow recommended practices given on the
label for use and disposal of pesticides and pesticide containers.

Acknowledgments

Thanks go to Vincent D'Amico for providing the cover artwork.

Proceedings
16th U.S. Department of Agriculture
Interagency Research Forum on Gypsy Moth
and Other Invasive Species
2005

January 18-21, 2005
Loews Annapolis Hotel
Annapolis, Maryland

Edited by
Kurt W. Gottschalk

Sponsored by:

Forest Service Research

Agricultural Research Service

Animal and Plant Health Inspection Service

Cooperative State Research, Education and Extension Service

FOREWORD

This meeting was the sixteenth in a series of annual USDA Interagency Gypsy Moth Research Forums that are sponsored by the USDA Gypsy Moth Research and Development Coordinating Group. The title of this year's forum reflects the inclusion of other invasive species in addition to gypsy moth. The Committee's original goal of fostering communication and an overview of ongoing research has been continued and accomplished in this meeting.

The proceedings document the efforts of many individuals: those who made the meeting possible, those who made presentations, and those who compiled and edited the proceedings. But more than that, the proceedings illustrate the depth and breadth of studies being supported by the agencies and it is satisfying, indeed, that all of this can be accomplished in a cooperative spirit.

USDA Gypsy Moth Research and Development Coordinating Group:

Kevin Hackett, Agricultural Research Service (ARS)
Vic Mastro, Animal and Plant Health Inspection Service (APHIS)
Bob Nowierski, Cooperative State Research, Education and Extension Service (CSREES)
Robert Bridges, Forest Service-Research (FS-R), Chairperson

Acknowledgments
The program committee would like to thank The Heron Group, LLC, Hercon Environmental, Arborjet, Inc., JJ Mauget Company, and the Management and Staff of the Loews Annapolis Hotel for their support of this meeting.

Program Committee:
Mike McManus, Kevin Thorpe, Vic Mastro, Joseph Elkinton, and Barbara Johnson

Local Arrangements:
Kathleen Shields, Katherine McManus

Proceedings Publication:
Kurt Gottschalk

Contents

ASSESSMENT OF THE RISK OF INTRODUCTION OF *ANOPLOPHORA GLABRIPENNIS* IN MUNICIPAL SOLID WASTE FROM THE QUARANTINE AREA OF NEW YORK CITY TO LANDFILLS OUTSIDE OF THE QUARANTINE AREA: A PATHWAY ANALYSIS OF THE RISK OF SPREAD AND ESTABLISHMENT

Alan N.D. Auclair[1], G. Fowler[1], M.K. Hennessey[1], A.T. Hogue[2], M.A. Keena[3], D.R. Lance[4], R.M. McDowell[2], D.O. Oryang[2] and A.J. Sawyer[4]

[1] USDA-APHIS-PPQ, Center for Plant Health Science and Technology, Pest Epidemiological Risk Analysis Laboratory, 1730 Varsity Dr., Raleigh, NC 27606
[2] USDA-APHIS, Policy and Program Development, Risk Analysis Systems, 4700 River Rd., Unit 117, Riverdale, MD 20737
[3] USDA-FS, Northeastern Center for Forest Health Research, Northeastern Research Station, 51 Mill Pond Rd., Hamden, CT 06514
[4] USDA-APHIS-PPQ, Center for Plant Health Science and Technology, Otis Research Laboratory, Bldg. 1398, Otis ANGB, MA 02542

Abstract

The risk associated with spread of Asian longhorned beetle, *Anoplophora glabripennis* (Motschulsky) (ALB), from infested areas in New York City (NYC) to the wide array of landfills across the eastern United States contracted by the city since 1997 was unknown, but of great concern. Landfills (some as far away as South Carolina, Virginia, and Ohio) occupied forest types and climates at high risk of Asian longhorned beetle establishment. The city proposed a separate waste wood collection estimated to cost federal and state agencies $6.1 to $9.1 million per year, including the cost of processing and disposal of the wood. Pathway analysis was used to quantify the probability that Asian longhorned beetles present in wood waste collected at curbside would survive transport, compaction, and burial to form mated pairs. The study found that in seven alternate management scenarios, risks with most pathways are very low, especially given existing mitigations. Mitigations included chemical control, removal of infested trees, and burial of wood waste in managed landfills that involved multiple-layering, compaction, and capping of dumped waste with a 15-cm soil cover at the end of each day. Although the risk of business-as-usual collection and disposal practices was virtually nil, any changes of policy or practice such as illegal dumping or disposal at a single landfill increased the risk many thousand fold. By continuing and/or increasing the control and eradication of ALB, thus reducing the potential numbers of beetles on the pathway, the risk can be even further reduced while rigorously maintaining the same disposal practices and saving the taxpayers millions of dollars.

SIREX NOCTILIO (HYMENOPTERA: SIRICIDAE)—THE NEW ZEALAND EXPERIENCE

John Bain

Forest Biosecurity and Protection, Forest Research, Private Bag 3020, Rotorua, New Zealand

Abstract

Sirex noctilio F. is a wood wasp that is widely distributed in the Palearctic region. It has become established in New Zealand (first record 1900), Australia (1952), Uruguay (1980), Argentina (1985), Brazil (1988), South Africa (1994) and Chile (2001). The usual hosts are *Pinus* spp. but sometimes *Abies, Larix, Picea* and *Pseudotsuga* spp. are attacked. The wasp oviposits in the trunks of live trees (and moribund trees and logs) and at the same time deposits a phytotoxic mucus and arthrospores of *Amylostereum areolatum* (Fries) Boidin into the wood. The mucus kills the sapwood tissues and as the wood dries out it becomes suitable for the growth of the fungus. The *Sirex* larvae tunnel through the wood and derive their nourishment from the fungus. Susceptible trees may be killed.

No serious *Sirex* damage in New Zealand was noted until the 1920s; between 1946 and 1951 serious outbreaks were associated with extreme drought conditions and overstocked stands. In the central North Island 33% of trees were killed over an area of about 120,000 hectares. In the main it was sub-dominant and suppressed trees that succumbed, but in many areas dominant (crop) trees died as well.

In 1928-29 and 1931 *Rhyssa persuasoria* (L.) (Ichneumonidae) was deliberately introduced from Europe as a control measure. It was first recovered from the field in 1936 and is well established in nearly all exotic pine plantations. In 1956 *Rhyssa lineolata* (Kirby), a Nearctic species, was found in New Zealand and probably entered the country in timber cut from *Sirex* infected trees; the host siricid could not have been *S. noctilio* because this species does not occur in the Nearctic. *R. lineolata* is now found in several exotic forests. *Ibalia leucospoides* (Hockenwarth) (Ibaliidae) was introduced in 1950, 1951 from England and again in 1966-68 from Australia (the original source was California). It was first recovered in 1957 and is well established throughout the country. *Megarhyssa nortoni* (Cresson) (Ichneumonidae) was introduced from the USA between 1962 and 1964 and was first recovered from the field in 1968; it is now widespread. This complex of introduced parasitoids may kill over 70% of *Sirex* larvae in particular forest areas and in some localities *M. nortoni* has achieved parasitism rates of about 90%.

In the 1960s several other parasitoid species, mainly species of *Rhyssa* and *Megarhyssa*, were imported but for various reasons no liberations were made.

In 1962 *Deladenus siricidicola* Bedding (Neotylenchidae), a nematode associated with *Sirex*, was first found in New Zealand. It has subsequently been found in Europe and must have come from there in *Sirex* infested timber. The nematodes feed on the *Amylostereum* fungus in *Sirex* infested wood but and when they come close to a *Sirex* larva they change into an "infective form" and penetrate the integument of the larva. When an infected female larva pupates, the nematodes migrate to the ovaries and penetrate the eggs rendering them sterile. The nematodes also enter the testes of the male *Sirex* but this infection does not result in sterility. The nematode can be cultured on wheat inoculated with *Amylostereum* and it has been introduced in plantations where it does not occur naturally in an agar-based medium. The nematode often causes 90% of emerging *Sirex* females to be sterile.

The combined effect of the nematode, the introduced insect parasitoids and improved silviculture, resulting in more vigourous stands of trees, has kept *Sirex* populations in New Zealand at a very low level and today it is considered to be a minor problems with just the occasional flare up in activity in isolated stands that are under extreme stress, usually as a result of overstocking due to lack of timely thinning regimes.

The biological control of *Sirex*, not only in New Zealand but elsewhere, has been an excellent example of cooperation between several countries including Argentina, Australia, Brazil, Chile, United Kingdom, USA and Uruguay.

ANALYSIS OF mtDNA SEQUENCE DATA FOR THE ASIAN LONGHORNED BEETLE (*ANOPLOPHORA GLABRIPENNIS*): EVIDENCE FOR MULTIPLE INVASIONS IN NORTH AMERICA

Maureen E. Carter[1], E. Richard Hoebeke[1], Richard G. Harrison[2], Steven M. Bogdanowicz[2], Melody Keena[3] and Alan Sawyer[4]

[1]Department of Entomology, Cornell University, Ithaca, NY 14853
[2]Department of Ecology and Evolutionary Biology, Cornell University, Ithaca, NY 14853
[3]USDA Forest Service, Northeastern Center for Forest Health Research, Hamden, CT 06514
[4]USDA-APHIS-PPQ, Otis Plant Protection Laboratory, Otis ANG Base, MA 02542

Anoplophora glabripennis (Motschulsky), known as the Asian longhorned beetle (ALB) in the United States, is an invasive forest pest. This wood-boring beetle, first detected in New York City in 1996, in Chicago in 1998, in Toronto in 2003, and in New Jersey in 2002 and 2004, was accidentally introduced to the United States in solid wood packing materials and is a significant threat to our urban and natural forests.

Sequence data from mitochondrial COI and COII were edited and trimmed to 1645 characters. Data analysis was carried out with PAUP 4.0b10 using neighbor joining. All characters were weighted equally.

The mtDNA haplotype of beetles from Carteret, NJ differed from that of New York City/Jersey City beetles by 18 nucleotide sites, from that of Toronto beetles by 17 nucleotide sites, and from the Chicago/New York City mtDNA haplotype by 4 nucleotide sites. Ranking them in terms of genetic distance from the New York City/Jersey City, population, we have the Chicago/New York City mtDNA haplotype most similar (4 different nucleotide sites) followed by the Toronto mtDNA haplotype (7 different nucleotide sites) followed by the Carteret mtDNA haplotype (18 nucleotide sites) as indicated by clade distances.

We show that beetles from the Toronto and Carteret populations each has its own unique mtDNA haplotype. This suggests that these invasions were initiated separately from each other and from the primary New York/Jersey City invasion. This data does not support the hypothesis that beetles dispersed from New York City/ Jersey City to Carteret.

All of the Jersey City beetles share only one of the two mtDNA haplotypes found in the New York City beetles. This might indicate that one or only a few beetles spread from one of the populations in Queens to found the Jersey City population, and that it was not a separate introduction event.

We can say that two distinct haplotypes invaded New York. They must have been introduced from distinct source populations or from one heterogeneous population. Research is ongoing to sample potential source populations across China and Korea.

COMPARING SYSTEMIC IMIDACLOPRID APPLICATION METHODS FOR CONTROLLING HEMLOCK WOOLLY ADELGID

Richard S. Cowles[1], Carole S.- J. Cheah[1] and Michael E. Montgomery[2]

[1]Connecticut Agricultural Experiment Station
[2]Northeastern Research Station, USDA Forest Service, Hamden, CT

Several studies have shown imidacloprid to have excellent activity for controlling hemlock woolly adelgid (HWA) in a landscape environment (Cowles and Cheah 2002, Doccola et al. 2003, Webb et al. 2003). This study was undertaken to determine which imidacloprid application method would provide the best control of HWA in forests. The methods compared were Kioritz soil injection with (1) placement near the trunk; or (2) placement near the trunk and out to the drip line; (3) drench near the base of the trunk with Bayer Tree and Shrub Insect Control; and trunk injection with the (4) Arborjet, (5) Wedgle, and (6) Mauget systems. Along with the untreated check, these treatments were part of a 7 × 2 factorial design, which included a comparison of fall vs. spring application timing.

Trees were chosen for this study based on the presence of moderate populations of HWA, the availability of lower branches from which adelgid populations could be observed, and a distance of at least 50 m between study trees. Six replicates were located at five sites in Connecticut: Shenipsit State Forest in Somers, Nathan Hale State Forest in Coventry, Tunxis State Forest in East Hartland, Sequassen Boy Scout Camp in New Hartford, and the Mashantucket Pequot Reservation in Ledyard, for a total of 84 study trees. Insecticides were applied between October 1-29, 2002 and between May 28 - June 6, 2003. The Kioritz-injected imidacloprid treatments used Merit 75W and 1 g of active ingredient per 2.5 cm DBH. Bayer Advanced Tree and Shrub Insect Control (68 ml of product per 2.5 cm DBH, providing 1 g a.i.) was diluted in 3.8 liters of water and drenched outwards from the trunk of the tree to a distance of 45 cm. Trunk injection applications were made of Mauget's Imicide (3 ml of 10% formulation per 15 cm circumference), Wedgle's Pointer (1 ml of 12% formulation every 10 cm circumference), and Arborjet's Imajet (6 ml of 5% formulation every 24 cm circumference) while following each manufacturer's recommended method. The targeted dosages for the Mauget, Wedgle, and

Arborjet systems were 0.15, 0.09, and 0.1 g a.i./2.5 cm DBH, respectively. The application rate in the fall with the Wedgle System could not be confirmed, as there is no component to the application device that permits monitoring of active ingredient placement in the tree. Therefore, plugging of the needle orifice (a common occurrence) led to squeezing the handles without actually placing any product in the tree. Two modifications of the Wedgle method were required for successful springtime trunk injections. To prevent plugging of the needle orifice, a 7/64-inch hole was drilled into the center of the hole left by the bark corer. The injection plug was then inserted as before, and the needle inserted through the plug into the small diameter hole. Unlike the fall application, the application in the spring resulted in easily observable separation of the bark at the cambium layer where imidacloprid suspension was being deposited. Weighing the insecticide reservoir bottle before and after application with a portable electronic centigram balance allowed determination of the amount of product injected into each tree. Calibration marks on the Wedgle device were found to not correctly represent the volume of liquid being injected into the tree, so additional pressurizations (four per injection site) were used to compensate.

Cold temperatures during the winter resulted in mortality at study sites in nearby untreated trees of 85 - 95%. Therefore, mortality was not evaluated for the overwintering generation but delayed until July 7-15 when following (progrediens) had developed. Mortality was also assessed in late November 2003, and mid-December 2004. In July, shoots with adelgids were brought back to the laboratory in a cooler and evaluated under a dissecting microscope. Adelgids were probed to determine whether there was movement of legs or mouth parts, and the numbers of living and dead adelgids were counted from a sample of 100 individuals per tree. In the November and December assessments, 5 shoots were cut from the lower canopy, and 5 shoots from a height of 20 - 30 feet. Adelgids were counted on each shoot, up to a total of ten adelgids per shoot. The total for the 10 samples then constituted a 1 - 100 infestation rating.

We used an immunological method to measure imidacloprid residues (EnviroLogix, 2003) to compare with mortality data. Sap from hemlock branches was expressed from 20 - 50 cm long shoots on May 2 - 6, July 7 - 15 and August 20 - 27, 2003, using a hyperbaric chamber pressurized to ~200 p.s.i. with nitrogen. Sap collected with a pipette required no additional clean-up procedure before being tested with the EnviroLogix ELISA kit. Volumes of 250 - 700 μl were obtained for each sample with 100 μl required for imidacloprid determination. Sap samples were kept frozen once they were brought to the lab.

Results and Discussion

Site variability and natural mortality affected adelgid survival and obscured insecticide treatment effects in the July assessment. Adelgid mortality ranged from an average of 64% for the Wedgle-treated trees to 80% for the Kioritz, near trunk imidacloprid placement. Adelgids in the untreated check trees experienced 69% mortality.

November 2003 and December 2004 evaluations of adelgid populations determined that fall and spring application timing did not significantly differ. The November 2003 evaluations determined that soil applications resulted in an average population suppression of 79% relative to the untreated check. The Kioritz near-trunk placement of Merit in the fall of 2002 resulted in 100% mortality of adelgids as measured 13 months later. Suppression of adelgids with the soil applications improved further over the next year, resulting in an average of 98.5% reduction compared to the untreated check. Four of the six treatment combinations for soil application resulted in non-detectable HWA populations on the treated trees 18 - 26 months post-treatment.

In contrast to the soil applications of imidacloprid, trunk injections did not result in significant reductions in adelgid populations, either in the 2003 or 2004 evaluations. Of the trunk injection methods, the Mauget system resulted in populations that were intermediate in value and not significantly different from either the untreated check or the soil application treatments.

The ELISA assay of sap indicated that soil-based application of imidacloprid resulted in good mobilization and persistence in branches. With the Mauget system injections, a relatively short-lived, highly concentrated peak of imidacloprid was found in sap of some branches. Residues from the other two trunk injection methods were of low concentration.

The Mauget System allows visual monitoring of uptake of the formulated product into the tree—however, on many occasions the 3 ml capsules did not empty into the tree and had to be removed in spite of the lack of uptake. Capsules are pressurized, so any material not taken into the tree was lost onto the bark of the tree when the feeder tube was removed, making accurate measurement of uptake impossible. Uptake was very poor in the spring, and better, but variably successful, in the fall.

The Arborjet System provided the most complete feedback to operators regarding the movement of insecticide into the tree at the time of injection. Both the ability of the tree to accept the formulated product and the volume of product applied are easily monitored: the first through the pressure gauge attached to the injection needle, and the second through the injection reservoir calibrated in milliliters.

The imidacloprid test kits have proved to be an effective method for analysis of residues from hemlock sap. Concentrations can be quantified from 0.5 - 5 ppb, requiring considerable dilution and repeat testing for higher concentration samples. Nonspecific binding results in values of imidacloprid from sap ranging up to 5 ppb, so at least a 1:10 dilution is required and quantitation of imidacloprid below 5 ppb is not possible with this method. The results have to be considered as semi-quantitative for imidacloprid because some of its metabolites are also detected (though to a lesser degree than the parent compound). It is adaptable for analysis of tissue (needle and twig) samples and the results can be read with a relatively inexpensive scanner and image measurement software.

Summary

Trunk injection methods were less effective for control of HWA than near-trunk soil placement of imidacloprid. Efficacy of injections might be improved if the resulting short duration of mobilization in sap is timed to closely match peak feeding activity of adelgids (e.g., mid-April). The soil applications resulted in long-term moderate concentrations of imidacloprid in the sap, which may be responsible for the reliable, highly effective suppression of HWA populations. The ability of soil application of imidacloprid to provide multiple-year control of HWA must be balanced with the cost of this treatment and its potential to harm non-target aquatic organisms. Analyses of hemlock tissue foliage on untreated trees in this study determined that significant lateral and down-slope movement of imidacloprid can occur when imidacloprid is applied in water-saturated forest soil (data not shown). Insecticide treatment should be considered a stop-gap measure to preserve trees that are of exceptional value until such time that biological control becomes established.

Acknowledgments

We would like to thank Rose Hiskes and Mary Frost for technical assistance, and Brad Onken and the U.S. Forest Service Forest Health Management program for supporting this research. This work was funded through grant #03-CA-11244225-187, awarded by the Northeastern Area State and Private Forestry, USDA Forest Service.

Disclaimer

Use of a product name does not imply endorsement of the product to the exclusion of others that may also be suitable.

References

Cowles, R.S. and C.A. S.-J. Cheah. 2002. **Systemic control of hemlock woolly adelgid, 1999.** Arthropod Management Tests 27: G47.

Doccola, J.J., Wild, P.M., Ramasamy, I., Castillo, P. and Taylor, C. 2003. **Efficacy of Arborjet VIPER microinjections in the management of hemlock woolly adelgid.** J. Arboric. 29: 327-330.

Envirologix. 2003. www.envirologix.com/library/ep006spec.pdf

Webb, R.E., Frank, J.R. and M.J. Raupp. 2003. **Eastern hemlock recovery from hemlock woolly adelgid damage following imidacloprid therapy.** J. Arboric. 29: 298-302.

FUEL CHARACTERISTICS OF NONNATIVE INVASIVE PLANTS IN FORESTS OF THE NORTHEASTERN AND MID-ATLANTIC U.S.A.

Alison C. Dibble and Catherine A. Rees

USDA Forest Service, Northeastern Research Station, 686 Government Rd., Bradley, ME 04411
adibble@earthlink.net

Abstract

Nonnative invasive plants have severe consequences for ecosystems. In Northeastern and mid-Atlantic states, Japanese barberry (*Berberis thunbergii*), Asian bittersweet (*Celastrus orbiculatus*), Asian honeysuckle (*Lonicera* spp.), and Norway maple (*Acer platanoides*) are among many species that encroach in native forests and openings. Some can outcompete native vegetation, change soil chemistry and hydrology, degrade habitat for wildlife, and alter fuels that a wildfire might consume. But how do these plants interact with fire in this region? A long record of both small and large wildfires belies the popular assumption that fire is of little consequence here. Typically wildfires in the region are associated with extended drought. A prominent example is October 1947 in Maine, when more than 213,000 ac burned, with losses of 851 year round and 395 seasonal residences in 35 towns.

Presence of nonnative invasive plants might alter a fuelbed in one of two ways. An invaded forest is either more likely to burn, or less likely. In most forest types in our region, fuels that include invasive plants might lead to greater potential for wildfire. At one of our study sites, Acadia National Park in Bar Harbor, ME, early successional forests developed after the 1947 fires. The latter case is detrimental in pitch pine forests such as at Albany Pine Bush Preserve, Albany, NY, because this fire-adapted ecosystem requires occasional fire to keep the pitch pine as the dominant tree species. Understory plants and a rare butterfly, the Karner blue (*Lycaeides melissa samuelis*), depend on fire to maintain the native community.

We compared invaded and uninvaded forest stands at 13 sites in MA, MD, ME (including Acadia National Park), NJ, NY, VA, and VT, mostly on public lands (Table 1).

We also examined forest regeneration (woody plant seedlings) relative to invaded conditions as an indication of future forest conditions. Uninvaded conditions were to be as much like the invaded stands as possible, with mature forest and no invasives, and were to represent conditions toward which managers would seek to restore degraded stands. Given the best of what was available, few of our supposedly uninvaded stands were free of nonnative plants.

Using nonparametric tests, we found several patterns: (1) in three pitch pine sites, basal area was lower in uninvaded stands, and fire return interval could be influenced by invading, nonflammable black locust (*Robinia pseudoacacia*) and by exotic grasses; (2) in ten sites with various cover types other than pitch pine, mass of nonwoody litter in tons/acre and duff depth are greater in uninvaded stands, and basal area is lower, while mass of 100 hour fuels (> 7.5 cm diameter) is lower. Where present, nonnative grasses (e.g., fine-leaved sheep fescue, *Festuca filiformis*; sweet vernal grass, *Anthoxanthum odoratum*; wood blue grass *Poa nemoralis*) increase the load of fine fuels (Fig. 1), suggesting that during an extreme drought in autumn, wildfire could spread more easily than it would in a forest stand where grasses are not present. In general, seedlings of native woody plants were more abundant where invasive shrubs were lacking, while seedlings of invasive shrubs were dense in some of the invaded stands, with > 400 seedlings per sq m in some cases. A nonnative shrub, alder buckthorn (*Frangula alnus*), was especially dense in some sites and is a potential competitor of northern red oak and other native hardwoods. It appears that a control program that targets woody plants but neglects the encroachment by invasive grasses might not relieve the buildup of nonnative fine fuels.

Table 1.—Study sites in which we measured fuels in invaded (i) and nearby uninvaded (u) forest conditions. Abbreviations in Column 1 identify study sites in Figure 1.

Site	Location	Total ha	Cover	Forest Type designation	Target invasives
Acadia National Park (AC)	Bar Harbor, Hancock Co., ME	14,165	Poplar sp. (i) Red oak/red spruce (u)	Hardwoods	Ninebark and shrubby St. Johnswort
Albany Pine Bush Preserve (AF)	Albany, Albany Co., NY	809	Black locust (i) (u)	Pitch pine	Black locust
Albany Pine Bush Preserve (AL)	Albany, Albany Co., NY	809	Black locust (i) (u)	Pitch pine	Black locust
Antietam National Battlefield (AN)	Antietam, Washington Co., MD	394	Oak/hickory hardwoods	Hardwoods	Japanese honeysuckle
Cape Cod National Seashore (CC)	Wellfleet, Barnstable Co., MA	17,647	Black locust (i) Pitch pine (u)	Pitch pine	Black locust
Finger Lakes National Forest (FL)	Hector, Schuyler Co., NY	6,221	Oak/hickory hardwoods	Mixed woods	Multiflora rose
Holbrook Island Sanctuary (HI)	Brooksville, Hancock Co., ME	498	Red spruce/ Balsam fir	Softwoods	Norway maple
Manassas National Battlefield Park (MA)	Manassas, Prince William Co., VA	2,024	Oak/hickory hardwoods	Mixed woods	Japanese honeysuckle
Merck Forest and Farmland Center (MK)	Rupert, Bennington Co., VT	1,275	Mixed hardwoods	Hardwoods	Asian honeysuckle
Massabesic Experimental Forest (ME)	Lyman, York Co., ME	1,488	Red oak - white pine	Mixed woods	Oriental bittersweet
Morristown National Historical Park (MO)	Morristown, Morris Co., NJ	686	Oak - yellow poplar hardwoods	Hardwoods	Japanese barberry
Penobscot Experimental Forest (PE)	Bradley, Penobscot Co., ME	1,538	Oak – poplar with softwoods	Hardwoods	Frangula alnus
Rachel Carson National Wildlife Refuge (RC)	Kittery, York Co., ME	1,902	Eastern white pine on old fields and mixed hardwoods	Softwoods	Japanese barberry

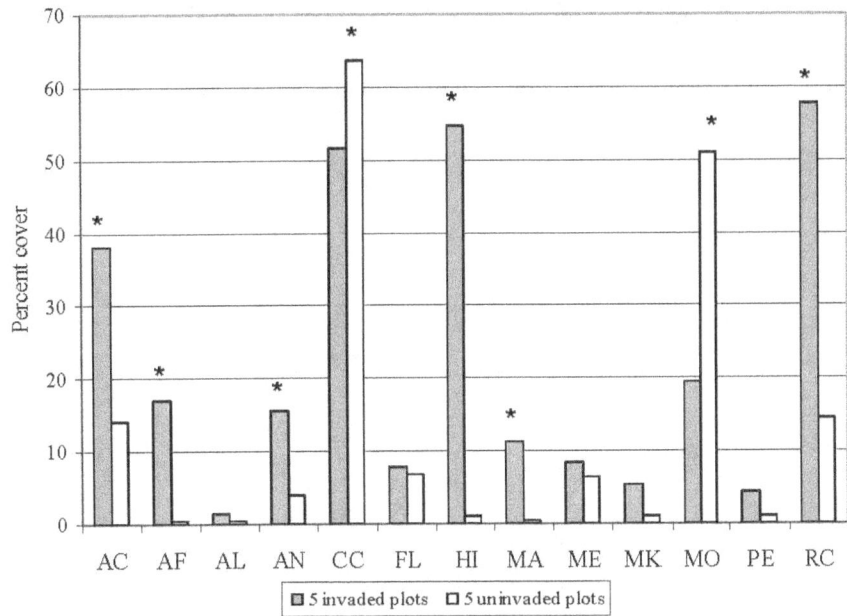

Figure 1.—Graminoid cover at 13 study areas. Values are average midpoint for Braun-Blanquet cover classes in five plots (3 m radius) per condition as invaded or uninvaded at each area. Abbreviations for sites are given in Table 1. AF, AL, and CC are fire-adapted pitch pine types. At CC, native *Carex pensylvanica* accounts for the graminoid abundance. * = significant at alpha=0.05 in two-group t-tests.

Acknowledgments

This study was funded by the Joint Fire Science Program, Boise, ID. We appreciate participation in all parts of this study from Co-Principle Investigator William A. Patterson III, University of Massachusetts, Amherst, MA and from Mark J. Ducey, University of New Hampshire, Durham, NH.

Related study - Julie Richburg, University of Massachusetts, Amherst, MA, has recently completed research on dynamics of total available carbohydrate in invasive plants in response to burning and cutting treatments. Contact: richburg@forwild.umass.edu.

References

Dibble, A.C., Catherine A. Rees, Mark J. Ducey, and William A. Patterson III. 2003. **Fuel bed characteristics of invaded forest stands.** Workshop Proceedings. Using fire to control invasive plants: What's New, What Works in the Northeast. Pp. 26-29. University of New Hampshire Cooperative Extension, Durham, NH. http://www.ceinfo.unh.edu/forestry/documents/WPUFCI03.pdf

Dibble, A.C., W.A. Patterson III, and Robert H. White. 2003. **Relative flammability of native and invasive exotic plants of the Northeastern U.S.** Workshop Proceedings. Using fire to control invasive plants: What's New, What Works in the Northeast. Pp. 34-37. University of New Hampshire Cooperative Extension, Durham, NH. http://www.ceinfo.unh.edu/forestry/documents/WPUFCI03.pdf

Richburg, J.A., A.C. Dibble, and W.A. Patterson III. 2001. **Woody invasive species and their role in altering fire regimes of the Northeast and Mid-Atlantic states.** Pp. 104-111 in K.E.M. Galley and T. P. Wilson (eds.). Proceedings of the Invasive Species Workshop: the Role of Fire in the Control and Spread of Invasive Species. Fire Conference 2000: the First National Congress on Fire Ecology, Prevention and Management. Misc. Publ. No. 11, Tall Timbers Research Station, Tallahassee, FL.

Additional reading: http://www.fs.fed.us/ne/durham/4155/fire/dibble2_jfsp.html

ARBORJET APPROACH AND USE OF STEM MICRO-INFUSION TREATMENTS FOR THE MANAGEMENT OF SPECIFIC INSECT PESTS AND PHYSIOLOGICAL DISEASES IN FOREST, LANDSCAPE AND PLANTATION TREES

Joseph J. Doccola, Peter M. Wild, Eric J. Bristol and Joseph Lojko

Arborjet, Inc., 70B Cross Street, Winchester, MA 01890

Abstract

Presented in four posters is a cross section of injection methodology by Arborjet, Inc. Poster #1 summarizes a study conducted in 2003-2004 to assess the efficacy of Arborjet's micro-infused IMA-jet (5% SL) with the Tree I.V. system in the management of hemlock woolly adelgid (*Adelges tsugae* Annand). In this study, sixteen (16) 41 cm HWA infested eastern hemlock (*Tsuga canadensis* Carriere) were injected with a 1.6mL per cm DBH rate (0.8 gm a.i./cm DBH) IMA-jet formulation of imidacloprid. Four 9-mm diameter Arborplugs (differential septa) were set into the active transport (xylem) tissues as the micro-infusion interface. Eight non-treatment trees served as controls. Evaluations were performed in the fall 2004. Eight 45-60cm branch samples were taken from the mid-canopy of the study trees. Five branchlets were cut from each twig sample. HWA mortality was determined by microscopic examination. Viable HWA/linear cm was calculated for each sample examined. Annual twig extension (last three years) was also measured as an indicator of hemlock health. Live HWA pressures on treated trees equaled 0.04/linear cm compared to 1.8/linear cm for untreated trees, a 45X reduction in HWA pressure. Percent mortality on treated trees equaled 89.3% compared to 37.9% for the controls. Treatment tree growth response was 5.78 cm versus 4.19 cm in the controls, a difference that has biologically significance.

Poster #2 summarizes the cooperative work with Michigan State University studying the efficacy of trunk injections in the treatment of Emerald Ash borer (*Agrilus planipennis* Fairmaire). Mean ELISA imidacloprid residues for Arborjet's 5% IMA-jet treated trees was 350 ppb versus 42 ppb for Mauget's 10% Imicide. EAB adults feeding assay was also conducted to assess the relative efficacy of the injected imidacloprid formulations. Populations of EAB were fed branches from injected trees at 15, 28, 49, 59 and 70 days. EAB adult mortality was consistently higher in Arborjet's 5% IMA-jet treated trees as compared to Mauget's 10% Imicide and/or controls. Observed mortality was highest at 49 days, resulting in 90% in Arborjet treated trees vs 50% for Mauget treated trees and 40% in the controls.

Poster #3 presents some of the plant health studies performed in the process of formulation development. Current studies include the response of chlorotic pin oak (*Quercus palustris* Muench) to MIN-jet Iron treatments. Of interest, are efficacy and duration; 3x, 6x and 9x dose rates were use to assay dose-rate responses. A Pin oak severity rating was developed as a tool to aid in the assays. Physiological disease presents a range of symptomology from mild leaf yellowing to severe interveinal chlorosis, canopy dieback, epicormic dieback and ultimately, death as carbohydrate storage is depleted. Assays of plant health response are scheduled in 2005, 2006 and 2007. In a study performed in London plane trees (*Platanus* x *Acerifolia*) susceptible to defoliation by anthracnose were injected with MIN-jet Copper and compared with two systemic fungicides that are labeled for trunk injection. In this unique study we are interested in tree health response despite the presence of the causal agent. In previous injection work, we observed trees superior recovery and higher health indices (including more rapid development of woundwood at the injection sites) compared to fungicide treatments.

Poster #4 illustrates the relative wound response in trees using Arborjet methodology. An digital assessment was developed to help the practitioner to rate wound response in trees. The scale uses a -1, 0 and +1 rating system, where "-1" indicates wounds sites with cracking, oozing, "0" indicates no observable response and +1 is indicative of wound closure. Three factors influence wound response, which are the tree species (including xylem anatomy and wood density), the nature of the physical injury (methodology) and the formulation used (relative phytotoxicity).

GETTING THE WORD OUT: FHTET AND INVASIVE.ORG COLLABORATIONS

G. Keith Douce[1], Richard Reardon[2], David J. Moorhead[3], Charles T. Bargeron, IV[4]
and Christopher W. Evans[5]

[1]Professor of Entomology, [2]Professor of Silviculture, [3]Technology Coordinator and [5]Invasive Species Specialist,
Bugwood Network, University of Georgia, Tifton, GA 31793
[2]USDA Forest Service, FHP/FHTET, Morgantown, WV 26505

Abstract

The USDA Forest Service, Forest Health Protection, Forest Health Technology Enterprise Team (FHTET) publishes several forest health publications each year. These are high quality, full-color and highly requested publications that are distributed through traditional channels. The full-color photographs makes these publications extremely popular and useful, but quite costly to produce.

However, many people have not been able to obtain desired numbers of copies for a variety of reasons including:

1) distribution problems

2) supplies being exhausted since they are costly to produce

3) simply because the target user groups are not aware of them

Collaboration between FHTET and the University of Georgia, Bugwood Network has resulted in:

1. Photographs and images in the FHTET publications available through Invasive.org (www.invasive.org) and Forestry Images (www.forestryimages.org)

2. Text of the publications available in a web-based searchable format

3. Users able to find and download only those pages, images and sections of interest on an "as-needed" basis

Through Invasive.org www.invasive.org, we have extended the information and images contained in several recent FHTET publications to audiences across the U.S. and around the world. Additional images and information on these and other topics are provided through Invasive.org.

Linking content from multiple sources in an integrated, user-friendly, web-accessible environment increases their availability and value. As of December 2004, Invasive.org and Forestry Images together made 23,000+ images from over 730 photographers available for educational uses in multiple jpeg downloaded resolutions.

PROGRESS AND PITFALLS IN THE BIOLOGICAL CONTROL OF SALTCEDAR (*TAMARIX* SPP.) IN NORTH AMERICA

Tom L. Dudley

Dept. of Natural Resource and Environmental Science, University of Nevada,
1000 Valley Rd., Reno, NV, USA 89512-0013
tdudley@cabnr.unr.edu

Abstract

The invasion of saltcedar (a.k.a. tamarisk; *Tamarix* spp.) in riparian areas of western North America has caused serious economic and environmental problems based on its high rate of water use, exacerbation of flooding and wildfire risks, and displacement of native riparian vegetation and associated wildlife (Dudley et al. 2000, Shafroth et al. 2005). Several species are involved in this invasion, but most infestations consist of a *T. ramosissima* Ledeb. x *T. chinensis* Lour. hybrid (Gaskin and Schaal 2002). This deciduous shrub/small tree expanded its range greatly during the early 1900s following regulation of rivers in the West, although infestations also occur in relatively undegraded ecosystems that are not regularly flooded. Tamarisk now infests between 0.5 to 0.8 million acres of primarily historic cottonwood-willow riparian woodlands, and its invasion continues across the range with annual economic losses estimated at between $127 and $291 million (Zavaleta 2000).

Because traditional mechanical and chemical control methods are expensive and risk collateral damage to sensitive ecosystems, a biological control program was developed by Dr. C. Jack DeLoach (USDA-ARS Texas)(DeLoach et al. 2004). In 1996 two specialist insects were approved by APHIS for release: the saltcedar leaf beetle (Chrysomelidae: *Diorhabda elongata* Brulle) from central Asia and a mealy bug (Pseudococcidae: *Trabutina mannipara* Hemprich and Ehrenberg) from the eastern Mediterranean region; a foliage feeding weevil (*Coniatus tamarisci* F.) was later approved and numerous other agents been tested. Our primary focus was on *Diorhabda*, which oviposits on the foliage, feeds selectively on tamarisk in the larval and adult stages, and pupation and adult over-wintering take place in the litter beneath tamarisk plants.

At about the same time as releases were to occur, the U.S. Fish and Wildlife Service discovered that the endangered southwestern willow flycatcher (*Empidonax traillii extimus* Phillips) was nesting in saltcedar in some locations. The program was delayed for Section 7 Consultation under the Endangered Species Act, despite evidence that reproductive output by birds nesting in saltcedar was much lower than by those nesting in native vegetation and systems dominated by saltcedar no longer supported flycatcher nesting (Dudley and DeLoach 2004). Research continued with the release of *Diorhabda* in 1999, but only within secure cages and avoiding Arizona and New Mexico where the willow flycatcher was using saltcedar (and where the mealybug was intended for release in warm desert sites). The cage trials in six other states showed that the leaf beetle would survive in most, but with life cycles attenuated from what was observed in their original Asian range. Following cage trials and implementation of a monitoring program to track ecosystem responses to saltcedar biocontrol, open releases of *Diorhabda* were conducted at eight of these sites in 2001 (Dudley et al. 2001).

Initial results were not promising, but in late summer 2002 heavy defoliation of plants was observed at our northern Nevada site on the lower Humboldt River. By scraping foliar tissue the leaf beetles cause tissue water loss and subsequent near-complete defoliation of target plants. Approximately 2 ha. were affected around the release point in 2002, with population expansion in 2003 to defoliate about 200 ha. area, and then roughly 20,000 ha. in 2004. However, plants produced new foliage after 3 - 6 weeks but with roughly 40% less foliar cover. Multiple defoliation events can occur within a single year because beetles exhibited two generations in 2003, and three generations with an earlier spring leaf flush in 2004.

In stands defoliated over 3 years, nearly all host plants have survived but live tissue volume declines further after each herbivory bout, such that these plants only have 1-10% live tissue recovery after this period.

Even without causing host mortality, biocontrol provides substantial benefits based on our early observations at the Humboldt River site. Sap-flow measurements of evapotranspiration indicated that groundwater losses are reduced by approximately 75% during the first year of herbivory, and substantially greater savings occur in subsequent years (R. Pattison, USDA-ARS Reno, unpub. data). There was also a marked increase in wildlife use of tamarisk vegetation colonized by leaf beetles. Habitat use by insectivorous birds, as measured by fecal counts per 'perch', increased greatly (23 vs. 1.4 specimens per perch) and deposits were comprised almost entirely of *Diorhabda* body parts. Observations of small mammal foraging on the beetles, which over-winter in aggregations in the litter, were common in this habitat that otherwise supports few wildlife resources in any season (W. Longland, USDA-ARS Reno, unpub. data). In addition, replacement vegetation is starting to increase as understory plant species benefit from reduction in canopy shading, from 90% to approximately 60% over 1 year (R. Pattison, unpub. data). The concern, however, is that replacement vegetation will be dominated by other invasive species such as perennial pepperweed (*Lepidium latifolium*) and Russian knapweed (*Acroptilon repens*), so ecosystem restoration should take a holistic approach toward managing all invasive species together in a coherent ecological strategy.

Lesser success with *Diorhabda* releases occurred at the other sites, with moderate establishment in Wyoming, Utah, Colorado and a second Nevada site; no establishment occurred south of approximately 38° N nor in coastal drainages of California (DeLoach et al. 2004). There are three factors that explain establishment failures:
1) developmental mis-matching related to daylength
2) poor use of a different target tamarisk species
3) predation by ants.

The introduced *D. elongata* population originated from 44° N in NW China, and in incubator studies entered reproductive diapause at a critical daylength of 14.5 hours (Bean et al. 2001). Thus, it is reproductive for over 3 months at some northern sites but at mid-latitude (37.1 °N at Owens Valley, CA) daylength exceeds 14.5 hours for only one month so beetles entered diapause in the middle of summer while plants were still growing. Besides drastically reducing potential for population growth, early diapause means beetles have not accumulated sufficient metabolic reserves to survive through the remaining warm season and the winter. Further south this critical daylength is never met so reproduction cannot occur. Populations in coastal drainages of central California also failed to establish, partly due to temperature and daylength problems but primarily because a different species of tamarisk, *T. parviflora*, is the common invader in these systems. When *T. parviflora* and *T. 'ramosissima'*, the more common hybrid form present in desert sites, were planted together at the Humboldt site, the leaf beetles completely defoliated *T. 'ramosissima'* but only utilized ca. 65% of the planted *T. parviflora*. Feeding and growth performance on *T. parviflora* was poor in laboratory tests as well, so we conclude that this eastern Mediterranean species is an unsuitable host for the central Asian beetle. Finally, the eastern Oregon study site (43.7° N) should have been well suited for leaf beetle establishment, but here densities of harvester-type ants (*Formica* spp.) were very high, with a mean distance between colonies of 13 meters. *Formica* ants are important predators of larvae and adults of *Diorhabda* (Herrera et al. 2001), explaining this failure.

To overcome these barriers to biocontrol establishment, we have imported additional geographic races or biotypes of *Diorhabda elongata* from across Eurasia and northern Africa, representing the range of latitudes of ecosystems invaded in North America. Eight populations are now in culture, having been tested to ensure safety from non-target impacts and to allow genotyping by D. Kazmer and J. Tracy (USDA-ARS Montana and Texas, respectively). Two are from China including a biotype from lower elevation where tamarisk growth periods are long, one from Kazakhstan, two from Uzbekistan, two from Greece and the lowest latitude population is from 34.4 °N in Tunisia. Currently five of these are in the open field: a Greek population in southern locations and in a far-west site, the low elevation China biotype near 38 °N in the western Great Basin, the Kazakhstan form in Utah and a trial release of an Uzbeki biotype in Texas (DeLoach et al. 2004). There remain questions about which biotypes are appropriate for introduction in different regions and for different host genotypes, and concern that public and agency pressure to release biocontrol agents quickly will result in inappropriate releases and subsequent biocontrol failures. Thus, we are conducting experimental cage releases of four biotypes at 2-degree intervals along a latitudinal gradient from eastern Oregon to southern New Mexico, with additional sites to incorporate the major tamarisk species. This work is supported by the USDA Forest Service Division of Forest Health Protection through the Ogden, Utah regional office, and will generate more reliable information for regional managers to target the correct agent biotypes in their areas. As for the problem with ant predation, another biocontrol agent is being considered that may be more resistant to predation. *Cryptocephalus sinaita* (Suffrian) is a foliage-feeding chrysomelid beetle with specificity similar to *D. elongata*, but which builds a 'defensive' case as a larva much like that of a caddisfly.

New delays have resulted from USDA-ARS concerns over the potential for non-target impacts to the native alkali heath (*Frankenia salina* Johnston), a prostrate rhizomatous plant found in salt marshes. Prior testing indicated that larvae could feed and develop on this plant, which is distantly related to the Tamaricaceae, but little oviposition occurred in pre-release host-range testing (Lewis et al. 2003). More recently, we planted *F. salina* at our Nevada site where extraordinarily high densities of both larval and adult *Diorhabda* fed to only a minor extent (<6% tissue damage) on *Frankenia* and did not oviposit on the plant. Plants continued growing with no substantial impact, indicating that there is little reason for concern about non-target impacts in the few localities where these two plant taxa are in close proximity (Dudley and Kazmer 2005).

As we anticipate a transition from the research to the implementation phase of the Saltcedar Biological Control Program, we are increasingly confident that tamarisk can be suppressed, if not eradicated, in most of its invasive range. Biodiversity and water resources will be enhanced by both the presence of biocontrol agents and by their facilitation of measurable recovery of riparian and wetland vegetation, particularly if hydrological management can be applied simultaneously to create more natural flow regimes in arid western ecosystems. However, positive responses will also depend upon improved cooperation among agencies so that invasive species management in 'natural areas' can move forward more effectively than has been the case in this program. A tendency in some agencies toward a 'zero-risk' approach to weed management has caused major delays and expenditure of tight resources. A more feasible approach involves better coordination and communication of information among researchers, administrators and regulators so that we can address misunderstandings and fears before they interfere with the management of invasive species in wildland ecosystems.

References

Bean, D., T. Chew, Li, B. & R.I. Carruthers. 2001. **Diapause in relation to the life history of *Diorhabda elongata* (Chrysomelidae), a Eurasian leaf beetle introduced as a biocontrol agent of saltcedar (*Tamarix* spp.)(abstract).** Entomol. Soc. America, San Diego.

DeLoach, C.J., R. Carruthers, T. Dudley & 18 others. 2004. **First results for control of saltcedar (*Tamarix* spp.) in the open field in the western United States.** Pp. 505-513. R. Cullen (ed.) XI Internat. Symp. on Biol. Control of Weeds, Canberra, Australia.

Dudley, T.L., C.J. DeLoach, J. Lovich and R.I. Carruthers. 2000. **Saltcedar invasion of western riparian areas: Impacts and new prospects for control.** Pp. 345-381. Trans. 65th No. Amer. Wildlife & Nat. Res. Conf., March 2000, Chicago.

Dudley, T.L., C.J. DeLoach, P.A. Lewis and R.I. Carruthers. 2001. **Cage tests and field studies indicate leaf-eating beetle may control saltcedar.** Ecol. Restoration 19: 260-261.

Dudley, T.L. and D.J. Kazmer. **Field assessment of the risk posed by *Diorhabda elongata*, a biocontrol agent for control of saltcedar (*Tamarix* spp.), to** a non-target plant, *Frankenia salina.* Biological Control (in press).

Dudley, T.L. and C.J. DeLoach. 2004. **Saltcedar (*Tamarix* spp.), endangered species, and biological weed control - can they mix?** Weed Technology 18: 1542-1551.

Gaskin, J.F. and B.A. Schaal. 2002. **Hybrid Tamarix widespread in U.S. invasion and undetected in native Asian range.** Proc. Natl. Acad. Sci. USA 99: 11256-11259.

Herrera, A.M., R.I. Carruthers, D. Dahlsten & T. Dudley. 2001. **Field studies of *Diorhabda elongata* (Coleoptera: Chrysomelidae) larval survivorship, a biocontrol agent introduced against saltcedar (*Tamarix ramosissima*). (abstract).** Ent. Soc. America, San Diego.

Lewis, P.A., J.C. Herr, T.L. Dudley, R.I. Carruthers and C.J. DeLoach. 2003. **Assessment of risk to native *Frankenia* shrubs from an Asian leaf beetle, *Diorhabda elongata deserticola* (Coleoptera: Chrysomelidae), introduced for biological control of saltcedars (*Tamarix* spp.) in the western United States.** Biol. Cont. 27: 148-166.

Shafroth, P.B., J. Cleverly, T.L. Dudley, J. Stuart, C. Van Riper and E.P. Weeks. 2005. **Saltcedar removal, water salvage and wildlife habitat restoration along rivers in the southwestern U.S.** Environmental Management (in press).

Zavaleta, E. 2000. **The economic value of controlling an invasive shrub.** Ambio 29: 462-467.

EARLY DETECTION AND RAPID RESPONSE PILOT PROJECT

Donald A. Duerr

USDA Forest Service, Forest Health Protection, 1720 Peachtree Road, NW, Room 816 N, Atlanta, GA 30309

Abstract

The Early Detection and Rapid Response Team is developing the framework for and implementing a national, interagency detection, monitoring, and response system for nonnative invasive forest species. Nonnative invasive species are one of Forest Service Chief Bosworth's "four threats" and the great level of interest and publicity that recent nonnative tree pests like Asian longhorned beetle, emerald ash borer, and sudden oak death have received stresses the importance and high-profile nature of this problem. The survey protocols that have been developed since this project's inception have been deemed successful as several exotic species new to North America have been detected via its methods. The project needs to expand to cover more high-risk sites and to target a greater number and variety of high-risk species that are not yet established in North America.

Background

In 2001, a Memorandum of Understanding was signed by the Forest Service (FS) and Animal and Plant Health Inspection Service (APHIS) that identifies agency invasive species responsibilities and areas of coordination. In the same year, an Early Detection and Rapid Response Team was established to coordinate pilot tests for the detection of nonnative bark beetles and the nun moth. Team members include the Oregon Department of Agriculture, Maryland Department of Agriculture, Cornell University, Agricultural Research Service, APHIS, USFS Forest Health Protection, and other agencies, universities, and environmental groups as their cooperation is needed.

Team objectives include:

- Developing and testing a prototype national survey
- Identifying potential exotic pests and likely pathways
- Identifying detection and management guidelines
- Detecting and monitoring new introductions at selected high-risk sites
- Developing recommendations to address gaps in detection protocols and taxonomic resources
- Using the information collected to set agency protocols and priorities

Ten nonnative bark beetle species were specifically targeted, although all bark beetles captured were identified. The target species are among the most common and threatening species intercepted during port inspections. Good survey techniques (highly attractive lures and effective traps) exist for these species, although they are difficult taxonomically, which limits the number of samples we can process.

Overview

Each year since 2001, baited funnel traps (to capture bark beetles) have been placed in urban forests and forests around port facilities and wood-handling facilities in the following regions: northeastern/midwestern, southeastern, and western U.S. Trapping has been done in approximately 12 cities each year (over 40 cities to date). Over 3,000 samples from these traps have been collected, processed, and identified by three professional taxonomists. In 2001, nun moth detection surveys were performed at several port cities in the northeastern U.S. and the pacific northwest. These surveys were negative.

Highlights

In 2001, *Hylurgops palliatus*, a targeted species, was caught near Erie, PA; this represents a first-time detection in North America. Early Detection continues to pursue trapping to delimit the extent of establishment of *H. palliatus* in the area around southeastern Lake Erie. Also in 2001, *Arhopalus pinetorum*, a longhorned beetle, was detected for the first time in North America at Long Beach, CA.

In 2002, the pilot tests detected two more nonnative bark beetles for the first time in North America: *Xyleborus similis* in Houston, TX, and *Xyleborus glabratus* in Port Wentworth, GA. *H. palliatus* was found at multiple additional sites in northwestern Pennsylvania.

In 2003, Early Detection traps near Denver, CO and Ogden, UT trapped *Scolytus schevyrewi*, the banded elm bark beetle, for the first time in North America. Early Detection cooperated with APHIS to coordinate targeted detection/delimiting surveys throughout the west and midwest. As a result, *S. schevyrewi* has been found throughout the West and in several midwestern and eastern states. This species presents a potential risk to healthy and stressed elm trees. Early Detection facilitated and funded studies by Forest Service scientists to find the best attractant for this species and to assess its impacts.

Conclusions

The Early Detection Pilot Project demonstrated the feasibility of a regionally-coordinated national survey for bark beetles and, possibly, for other nonnative forest species. With additional funding and continued emphasis on exotic species, the pilot project can be expanded into a national program that will be a regular part of the survey efforts we support through the National Forests and state programs. This Early Detection program will represent a highly targeted detection and response effort that would enhance current FHP-supported surveys such as the aerial survey program, forest health monitoring, and species-specific trapping efforts to monitor populations of forest pests like the southern pine beetle and gypsy moth. The Early Detection program coordinates with and augments APHIS' CAPS program. Early detection data are located at: http://na.fs.fed.us/wv/rapid_det/.

Current and future focus areas to help the Early Detection and Rapid Response project expand and become more effective at detecting high-risk exotic species early enough to take eradication actions against them include: addressing the limiting taxonomy factor by training the field-level staffs who are doing the trapping to prescreen out the most common species and supporting new graduate students to learn taxonomy by processing Early Detection samples, continuing and refining the Early Detection database, developing new trapping methods to target other exotic species such as siricids, buprestids, and cermabycids, supporting the development of new screening and/or identification technologies, coordinating with the HFRA Title VI "Early Warning System", and cooperating with Forest Health Technology Enterprise Team and others on risk-rating for species and ecosystems.

DON'T LET CACTO BLAST US! : A COOPERATIVE EFFORT TO DETECT AND TEST CONTAINMENT OF THE CACTUS MOTH, *CACTOBLASTIS CACTORUM* (BERG) ON THE US GULF COAST

Joel Floyd[1], Kenneth A. Bloem[2], Stephanie Bloem[3], James E. Carpenter[4] and Stephen Hight[5]

[1]USDA, APHIS, PPQ, Pest Detection and Management Programs, 4700 River Rd., Unit 137, Riverdale, MD 20737
[2]USDA, APHIS, PPQ, CPHST, Florida A&M University, Tallahassee, FL 32307
[3]Center for Biological Control, Florida A&M University 6383 Mahan Dr., Tallahassee, FL 32317
[4]USDA, ARS, Crop Protection & Management Research Unit 2747 Davis Road, Tifton, GA 31794
[5]USDA-ARS, Center for Medical, Agricultural, & Veterinary Entomology 6383 Mahan Road, Tallahassee, FL 32317

The Cactus moth, *Cactoblastis cactorum* (Berg), showed its success in 1920s Australia as a biological control agent introduced to control invasive exotic prickly pear cacti, *Opuntia* spp. Subsequent introductions to other areas led to the Caribbean in the 1950s and a detection in the Florida Keys in 1989. The potential impacts of its U.S. spread includes effects on grazing, nursery and landscape industries and significant negative ecological impacts on hosts in deserts of the Southwestern U.S. Potential impacts in Mexico in addition to ecological include agricultural affects because of the importance of the fruit and cladodes for human consumption and forage.

The cactus moth spread along both Florida coasts in the 1990s and by 2004 on to Bull Island, SC on the Atlantic Coast and Dauphin Island, AL on the Gulf Coast. The cactus moth appears to be favoring barrier islands on the Gulf Coast and is currently not moving inland in the panhandle area of Florida. Dispersal rates along the coasts are approximately 160 kilometers/year, with an estimated arrival in Texas in the year 2004 barring artificial spread.

In cooperation with Mississippi State University's Georesources Institute, funded by the U.S. Geological Survey, a national detection network is being assembled to gather monitoring information from managed lands complementing state Cooperative Agriculture Pest Surveys. ARS and APHIS have been cooperating since 2000 on developing techniques for detection using an attractant, trap testing, mating studies, mass rearing on an artificial diet, and irradiated moth studies for application of the sterile insect technique (SIT). In the Spring of 2005, they will begin a large-scale SIT validation study on barrier islands in Florida and Alabama to ascertain whether a barrier can be established there to prevent the cactus moth's further westward movement.

EFFECTS OF PARENTAL AGE AT MATING ON THE REPRODUCTIVE RESPONSE OF THE GYPSY MOTH PARASITOID *GLYPTAPANTELES FLAVICOXIS* (HYMENOPTERA: BRACONIDAE)

R.W. Fuester[1], K.S. Swan[1], P.B. Taylor[1], and G. Ramaseshiah[2]

[1]USDA-ARS, Beneficial Insects Introduction Research 501 South Chapel Street, Newark, DE 19713
[2]377 Main 9, Cross 13, Vyalikaval Bangalore - 560003, India

Abstract

Glyptapanteles flavicoxis (Marsh) is an oligophagous, gregarious larval parasitoid of the Indian gypsy moth, *Lymantria obfuscata* (Walker), that readily attacks the European gypsy moth, *Lymantria dispar* (L.). This species is believed to have potential for inundative releases against gypsy moth populations, because it can be reared in large numbers with few hosts. Unfortunately, sex ratios in laboratory reared *G. flavicoxis* are usually male-biased. Male-biased sex ratios hinder efforts to mass release parasitic Hymenoptera for biological control by making the production of females costly. Because parental age at time of mating is known to affect the sex ratio in some Braconidae, we crossed haploid males and virgin females 0-, 1-, 4-, 9-, and 16-days-old with at least 10 trials for each of the 25 combinations. Numbers and sex ratios of progeny produced by females each day were recorded and subjected to two-way analysis of variance. We used the Holm-Sidak procedure to detect differences in sex ratios among progeny of differently aged parents and G-tests to test for treatment differences in proportions of females producing mixed and all male progeny. The numbers of progeny produced per female was positively correlated with female longevity. Both progeny and sex ratios (percent females) among progeny produced by ovipositing females of *G. flavicoxis* decreased markedly over time, so only the first days production need be used in mass rearing. The reduction in the proportion and numbers of females among progeny as ovipositing females aged is consistent with depletion of sperm in the spermatheca. Therefore, we focused our analyses on sex ratios in progeny produced on the first day hosts were provided to females. Females in all age classes mated to newly emerged males (day 0) were more likely to produce all male progeny (30%) than those mated to older males (10-15%). When crosses with only male progeny were excluded from the analysis, females mated to one-day-old males had higher sex ratios than those mated to males in other age classes. In addition, females mated the day that they emerged tended to have the highest sex ratios. Therefore, one should not use newly emerged males in rearing this species, but newly emerged females appear to be good candidates for a rearing program.

CELLULOSE DIGESTION IN THE LARVAE OF THE ASIAN LONGHORNED BEETLE (*ANOPLOPHORA GLABRIPENNIS*)

Scott Geib[1], Dan Jones[2], James Sellmer[3], Dean Morewood[1] and Kelli Hoover[1]

[1]Department of Entomology, The Pennsylvania State University, University Park, PA 16802
[2]Department of Chemistry, The Pennsylvania State University, University Park, PA 16802
[3]Department of Horticulture, The Pennsylvania State University, University Park, PA 16802

Abstract

In order for the Asian longhorned beetle (*Anoplophora glabripennis*) (ALB) to feed on the nutrient poor, inner wood of a host tree, we suspect that larvae have a cellulose digestion system. Cellulose digestion involves three enzyme components: (1) exoglucanases; (2) endo-glucanases; and (3) beta-glucosidases. In other insect species, cellulolytic enzymes are either endogenous or exogenous, either produced from symbiotic microbes maintained in the gut, or ingested through feeding.

The ability to digest cellulose was investigated in ALB larvae fed on artificial diet, a preferred host (*Acer sac*), and a resistant tree species (*Pyrus calleryana* var. Aristocrat). By incubating a gut homogenate with different cellulose substrates and measuring glucose production through a reducing sugar assay, enzyme activity of the three main enzyme components of the cellulase complex was identified in larvae fed sugar maple and callery pear, while reduced cellulase activity was detected in diet fed larvae. Based on the reducing sugar assay, the complete suite of cellulolytic enzymes was found in ALB fed on the preferred host (*A. sac*) with an average activity level of 0.65 µM glucose released/g gut/hr from crystalline cellulose. Larvae fed on the non-host (*P. calleryana* var. Aristocrat) retained the active cellulase enzyme complex. Enzyme activity levels showed no significant difference from maple-fed insects. This suggests that larval mortality in larvae fed on callery pear is not due to a disruption of the digestion system in the beetle. Larvae fed on artificial diet had a significant reduction in both beta-glucosidase and exoglucanase activities. This disruption in the cellulase complex was most likely due to the high level of simple sugar in the artificial diet (sucrose), suggesting that these cellulolytic enzymes are induced as needed during feeding. We also concluded that rearing on an artificial diet is not suitable to study digestion in this beetle. To our knowledge, this is the first report of the presence of a complete cellulase system in a cerambycid species that feeds on healthy trees.

THE ROLE OF TREE-FALL GAPS IN THE INVASION OF EXOTIC PLANTS IN FORESTS: THE CASE OF WINEBERRY, *RUBUS PHOENICOLASIUS*, IN MARYLAND

David L. Gorchov[1,2], Dennis F. Whigham[1], Anne F. Innis[1,3], Brianna Miles[1,4] and Jay O'Neill[1]

[1]Smithsonian Environmental Research Center, Edgewater, MD 21037
[2]Department of Botany, Miami University, Oxford, OH 45056
[3]Department of Biology, University of Maryland, College Park, MD 20742
[4]Department of Ecology, Evolution and Behavior, University of Minnesota, St. Paul, MN 55108

Abstract

In forests, plant invasions frequently begin in tree-fall gaps and other disturbed sites. Some forest invasives appear restricted to new gaps; others reach wide distributions within stands. Predicting the potential distribution of new invasives would be valuable for management. We propose that a forest invasive will be limited to newly disturbed sites if 1) establishment is limited to new disturbances, and 2) established individuals do not survive canopy closure. An invasive species that can either establish or persist under closed canopy has the potential to occupy the entire forest stand.

We evaluated the role of forest gaps in the invasion of *Rubus phoenicolasius* Maxim (Rosaceae), a native of Asia that is invasive in disturbed sites and successional forests in eastern USA. We censused 15 x 15 m plots centered in gaps created in a 2002 storm vs. random points in adjacent young and old deciduous stands at Smithsonian Environmental Research Center (38°53'N, 76°33'W), Maryland.

In the old stand, established *R. phoenicolasius* ramets were present in 10 of 20 gaps, but only 2 of 19 random plots. In large gaps ramet density was 34X greater, and primocane length double, compared to that in small gaps. Tip-rooting (vegetative reproduction) was limited to large gaps. In the young stand ramets were in all four gaps and four of five random plots. Fruits were present in three large gaps, but no small gap or random plots, in the old stand; in the young stand fruits were found in all gaps, but in only one random plot. In the mature stand seedlings were present in 10 gaps, but none of the random plots; seedling density was 4X in gaps associated with uprooted (vs. snapped) trees. In the young stand seedlings were present in three gaps and two random plots.

Thus, tree-fall gaps are required for seedling establishment, vegetative reproduction, and fruiting in mature forest. We are investigating whether established ramets persist with canopy closure in the forest and under different shade treatments in a garden experiment.

POTENTIAL FOR BIOLOGICAL CONTROL OF THE EMERALD ASH BORER

Juli Gould[1], Leah Bauer[2], Houping Liu[3], Dave Williams[1], Paul Schaefer[4] and Dick Reardon[5]

[1]USDA-APHIS, Pest Detection, Survey, and Eradication Laboratory, Otis ANGB, MA 02542-5008
[2]USDA Forest Service, North Central Research Station, 1407 S. Harrison Rd., East Lansing, MI 48823
[3]Department of Entomology, Michigan State University, E. Lansing, MI 48824
[4]USDA-ARS, Beneficial Insects Introduction Research Unit, 501 South Chapel Street, Newark, DE 19713-3814
[5]USDA Forest Service, Forest Health Technology Enterprise Team, 180 Canfield St., Morgantown, WV 26505

Abstract

The Emerald ash borer (EAB), *Agrilus planipennis*, is an invasive buprestid from Asia threatening North America's ash trees (*Fraxinus* spp.). Eradication of EAB in Michigan, although desirable, appears increasingly unlikely as managers discover a wide distribution of EAB throughout Michigan's Lower Peninsula and northern Ohio and Indiana. According to the National Management Plan for Invasive Species (National Invasive Species Council 2001), "When invasive species appear to be permanently established, the most effective action may be to prevent their spread or lessen their impacts through control measures. For certain invasive species, adequate control methods are not available or populations are too widespread for eradication to be feasible." We concur that integrated pest management methods, including the "release of selective biological control agents," are needed for control and management of EAB. Current containment efforts are critical to save our valuable ash resources while scientists develop rearing methods, perform safety testing, and conduct releases.

The results of studies conducted in Michigan since 2002, demonstrate that a variety of parasitoids attack EAB, including some that typically attack native *Agrilus* spp. (Bauer et al. 2005). Parasitism rates, however, are low (<1%) and clearly inadequate to suppress EAB populations below a density threshold for the survival of ash trees in Michigan. Entomopathogenic fungi resulted in ca. 2% mortality of EAB life stages under the bark. Predaceous beetles and woodpeckers also attack EAB in Michigan.

Emerald ash borer is reported from China, Mongolia, Japan, Korea, Russia, and Taiwan (Haack et al. 2002). During the past 2 years, scientists searched for EAB in each location except Taiwan. Although the type specimen of *A. planipennis* is from Mongolia, recent evidence suggests it was actually collected from Inner Mongolia in China (P. Schaefer). There appear to be few if any *Fraxinus* in Mongolia, thus, the prospects of collecting EAB natural enemies in that country are not promising. In Japan, *A. planipennis* subsp. ulmi is reported from the four main islands, with a host range of ash, elm (*Ulmus*), walnut (*Juglans*), and wingnut (*Pterocarya*) (Haack et al. 2002). Apparently EAB is rare and locally distributed in Japan, although a private collector secured a single EAB from ash after considerable effort (P. Schaefer). In South Korea, no EAB were found despite a month of searching that included applying sticky bands to girdled ash trees at nine locations; purple sticky traps; sweep netting for adults; and visual surveys for evidence of EAB-infested trees (D. Williams). In the Russian Far East, no *Agrilus* species were recovered from ash trees girdled at three sites in 2004 (V. Mastro).

We had considerably more success finding EAB in China. Working with cooperators from the Chinese Academy of Forestry (Dr. Yang Zhong-qi and Professor Gao Ruitong), surveys were conducted that successfully located populations of EAB in Heilongjiang, Jilin, Lianoning, and Hebei Provinces, as well as in Beijing and Tianjin City. EAB is typically at low density in China and is considered only a periodic pest of ash. Populations are probably maintained at low density by a combination of factors including host plant resistance and natural enemies.

Since 2002, several parasitoids of EAB were discovered in China. A new species of *Spathius* sp. (Hymenoptera: Braconidae) was found parasitizing EAB larvae in Jilin Province (H. Liu) and Tianjin City (Xu 2003). This gregarious ectoparasitoid paralyzes EAB larvae and deposits from 1 to 20 eggs per larva. The emergence of *Spathius* adults in the spring coincides with the

Table 1.—The characteristics of EAB parasitoids, and how they relate to the likelihood of successful biological control.

Characteristic	Probability for Biocontrol Success Higher	Spathius	Tetrastichus
Predator vs. Parasitoid	Parasitoid	Yes	Yes
# Generations per year	> 1 compared to host	Yes	Yes
Polyphagy	Monophagous	Unknown	Unknown
Sex Ratio	More Females	Yes (3:1)	Yes (2.5:1)
Oviposition Location	Oviposition on host	Yes	Yes
Internal Feeder?	Internal Feeder	No	Yes

presence of third and fourth-instar EAB larvae, which are the preferred host stages. This species also has four generations per year in Tianjin, and up to 90% parasitism was found in some ash stands (Yang et al. 2005). *Spathius* can be reared in the laboratory and host range studies in a quarantine facility in the U.S. are underway (J. Gould). A new species of *Tetrastichus* sp. (Hymenoptera: Eulophidae), a gregarious endoparasitoid, was found attacking EAB larvae in Heilongjiang, Jilin, and Liaoning Provinces; up to 50% EAB parasitism was found at one site in Jilin Province (Liu et al. 2003). This species has four generations per year (Yang Z.). Efforts to develop rearing methods for this *Tetrastichis* sp. are ongoing in a quarantine facility in the U.S. (L. Bauer and H. Liu). An undetermined species of *Sclerodermus* sp. (Hymenopetera: Bethylidae) attacks EAB pre-pupae (Yang Z. and R. Reardon), but parasitism levels are low. Female parasitoids enter overwintering chambers of EAB pre-pupae, remove frass, and deposit 15-20 eggs; ca. 70% of females are wingless, with limited dispersal capabilities. Members of this genus have also been known to sting humans, making this species unlikely to be approved for release. Egg parasitism has generally been low in China, but an egg parasitoid was discovered attacking EAB eggs in Jilin province: a new species of *Oobius* sp. (Hymenoptera: Encyrtidae) (Zhang et al. in press). This species reproduces parthenogenically and is currently being reared on EAB eggs in a quarantine facility in the U.S.; host range testing is planned (L. Bauer, H. Liu, R. Gao, and T. Zhao).

Predicting the potential for successful biological control of EAB cannot be done by investigating biocontrol success against other Buprestids. It is not that the projects were unsuccessful; it has simply not, to our knowledge, been attempted. We instead looked at how host-feeding niche and characteristics of the parasitoids might impact the probability of success. As the host-feeding niche becomes more concealed, e.g. from external feeders to leaf rollers/webbers to case-bearers, the average number of parasitoid species per host species increases from approximately six to twelve (Hawkins 1994). As the host becomes further concealed, however, the average number of parasitoid species drops to slightly over two in root feeders. Borers were found to support an average of four parasitoids species per host. A quick survey of *Agrilus* species in the United States (Solomon 1995) and Eurasia (Herting and Simmonds 1973) revealed an average of 3.6 and 4.0 parasitoids per host, respectively. There were certainly some *Agrilus* that supported more than four parasitoid species, however, this suggests that few additional EAB parasitoids will be discovered in China.

It is probable that one or more of the EAB natural enemies found recently in China will be useful biocontrol agents in North America. Kimberling (2004) reviewed characteristics of successful biological control agents and found that the most important traits are that the species is 1) a parasitoid, 2) multivoltine, and 3) monophagous. The qualities of *Spathius* and *Tetrastichus* fit the profile of a successful natural enemy (Table 1). Although we do not yet know if these parasitoids are monophagous, both have more than one generation per year, oviposit on the host, and have a sex-ratio skewed towards females. *Tetrastichus* is an internal feeder, while *Spathius* is not.

We anticipate the favorable characteristics of the parasitoid species, coupled with some preliminary evidence that North American ash species can withstand some level of EAB attack, will result in a successful reduction in the population levels and damage inflicted by the EAB.

References

Bauer, L.S., H. Liu, R.A. Haack, T.R. Petrice, and D.L. Miller. 2005. **Emerald ash borer natural enemy surveys in Michigan and China.** In Proceedings of the Emerald Ash Borer Research and Technology Development Meeting, Romulus, MI 10/5-6/2004 FHTET-2004-15 pp 71-72

Hawkins, B.A. 1994. **Pattern & Process in Host-Parasitoid Interactions.** Press Syndicate of the University of Cambridge, Cambridge, UK. 190 pp.

Haack, R.A., E. Jendek, H. Liu, K. Marchant, T. Petrice, T. Poland, and H. Ye. 2002. **The emerald ash borer: a new exotic pest in North America.** Michigan Ent Soc Newsletter 47:1-5. http://insects.ummz.lsa.umich.edu/MES/mes47n3%264.pdf

Herting, B. and F.J. Simmonds. 1973. **A Catalogue of Parasites and Predators of Terrestrial Arthropods. Section A. Volume III: Coleoptera to Strepsiptera.** Commonwealth Institute of Biological Control. 185 p.

Kimberling, D.N. 2004. **Lessons from history: predicting successes and risks of intentional introductions for arthropod biological control.** Biological Invasions 6: 301-318.

Liu, H., L.S. Bauer, R. Gao, T. Zhao, T.R. Petrice, and R.A. Haack. 2003. **Exploratory survey for the emerald ash borer, *Agrilus planipennis* (Coleoptera: Buprestidae), and its natural enemies in China.** Great Lakes Entomologist 36: 191-204.

Solomon, J.D. 1995. **Guide to insect borers of North American broadleaf trees and shrubs.** Agricultural Handbook 706. U.S. Department of Agriculture, Forest Service, Washington, D.C. 735 pp.

National Invasive Species Council. 2001. **National Invasive Species Management Plan.** http://www.invasivespecies.gov/council/actiond.shtml

Xu, G-T. 2003. *Agrilus marcopoli* **Obenberger**, pp. 321-322. In: G-T. Xu (ed.), Atlas of Ornamental Pests and Diseases. China Agriculture Press, Beijing, China. (in Chinese)

Yang, Z., J. S. Strazanac, P. M. Marsh, C. van Achterberg, and C. Won-Young. 2005. The first recorded parasitoid from China of the emerald ash borer: a new species of *Spathius* (Hymenoptera: Braconidae: Doryctinae). Annals of the Entomological Society of America. In press.

Zhang, Y-Z, D-W Huang, T-H Zhao, H-P Liu, and L. S. Bauer, 2005. **Two New Species of Egg Parasitoids (Hymenoptera: Encyrtidae) of Wood-Boring Beetle Pests from China.** Pytoparasitica. In Press.

A COMPARISON OF DIAPAUSE IN THE ASIAN AND NORTH AMERICAN GYPSY MOTH—IMPLICATIONS FOR POPULATION ESTABLISHMENT

David R. Gray[1] and Melody Keena[2]

[1]Natural Resources Canada, Canadian Forest Service, Atlantic Forestry Centre, 1350 Regent St., Fredericton, NB E3B 5P7
[2]USDA Forest Service, Northeastern Center for Forest Health Research, 51 Mill Pond Rd., Hamden, CT 06514-1777

Abstract

The Asian gypsy moth, *Lymantria dispar* L., (AGM) represents a significant threat to North America. In contrast to the North American strain (NAGM) that was introduced to the eastern U.S. circa 1868 (Liebhold et al. 1989) which feeds almost exclusively on deciduous hosts, and whose females are incapable of flight, the AGM has an extensive deciduous and coniferous host range, and females are strong fliers. Accidental introductions have occurred in British Columbia (1991), Washington (1997), Oregon (2000) and North Carolina (1993). Future introductions are virtually certain.

Successful establishment following an introduction has several requirements. Among these is that insect seasonality be satisfied. Seasonality is the predictable "occurrence of [a life stage event] within a definite limited period or periods of the astronomic (solar, calendar) year" (Leith 1974). Implicit in this definition for gypsy moth is that eggs will hatch coincidentally with the emergence of new foliage of host plants, that the cold-hardy, and low-temperature-requiring diapause phase (Leonard 1968, Gray et al. 2001) will coincide with winter, and that these events will coincide sufficiently each year for the continual survival of the population. Thus a multi-generational phenology model can directly assess one criterion of the risk of establishment of an introduced population to a new environment. It can make this assessment by quantifying the likelihood that temperature regimes in the environment will consistently produce seasonal development. Gray (2004) estimated the risk of establishment of the NAGM in this way. Before a similar estimation of the risk of establishment of the AGM can be done, the thermal requirements of diapause must be determined.

Keena (1996) showed that when eggs are exposed to various durations of 5 °C, a Russian population of AGM will hatch sooner than a NAGM population after the temperature is raised to 25 °C. The difference between strains increases as exposure duration decreases. As exposure duration decrease to 90d and lower, the hatch success of NAGM decreases sharply, whereas hatch of AGM is not noticably affected. This suggests that diapause requirments of AGM are more rapidly satisfied than those of NAGM at 5 °C. However, it is not sufficient information to construct the temperature-developmental rate relationships that are necessary for a phenology model.

As a first approximation to estimating the temperature developmental rate relationships in the AGM diapause we reared 30 AGM egg masses at 25 °C for 30d immediately after oviposition. This provided sufficient heat units to satisfy prediapause (Gray et al. 1991), and to initiate diapause, but not advance diapause development (Gray et al. 2001). We then divided each egg mass into 10 approx. equal samples and randomly assigned each of the 300 samples to one of 17 rearing treatments. Sixteen treatments each constituted a temporal sequence of

Table 1.—The number of days after diapause initiation that eggs were transferred to each temperature in the rearing regimetreatment.

Tk (°C)	treatments 1-4 transfer day				treatments 5-8 transfer day				treatments 9-12 transfer day				treatments 13-16 transfer day			
	7.5	Tk	7.5	25	7.5	Tk	7.5	25	7.5	Tk	7.5	25	7.5	Tk	7.5	25
-5	--	0	14	104	0	30	44	104	0	50	64	104	0	60	74	104
15	--	0	14	104	0	30	44	104	0	50	57	97	0	60	65	95
20	--	0	14	104	0	30	44	104	0	50	55	95	0	60	63	93
25	--	0	14	104	0	30	44	104	0	50	55	95	0	60	62	92

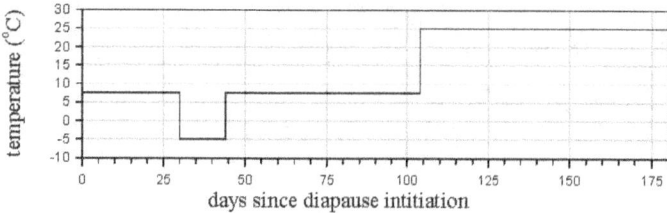

Figure 1.—Illustrates the temporal pattern of temperatures in the rearing treatment W2T1.

the temperatures shown in Table 1. Eggs in the 17th treatment served as a "control" and were reared at 7.5 °C for 90 d and then transferred to 25 °C. Thus all eggs received 90d at 7.5 °C between diapause initiation and transfer to 25 °C; eggs in the 16 treatments were also exposed to an "experimental" temperature for two to 14d. Figure 1 illustrates the temporal sequence of temperatures for the highlighted treatment of Table 1. The AGM strain was collected in the Russian far east near Mineralni (133°E, 44N°) and had been in quarantine at Hamden, CT for two generations.

Egg hatch was monitored thrice weekly, and daily percent cumulative egg hatch was calculated when egg hatch was completed. Daily percent cumulative diapause completion in each treatment was estimated by assuming that AGM post-diapause developmental rates and variability are equivalent to those observed in NAGM, and running the post-diapause model (Gray et al. 1995) in reverse to determine the number of individuals that likely completed diapause on each day. The functional relationships controlling diapause development were estimated by fitting the diapause model of Gray et al. (Gray et al. 2001) to the estimated dates of diapause completion. We assume that the putative mechanism governing developmental response in diapause is not different between the NAGM and the AGM, but that parameter values describing the relationships differ.

A comparison of the functional relationships controlling diapause is shown in Figure 2. Gray et al. (Gray et al. 2001) provided a detailed description of each parameter, and of the putative diapause mechanism. Briefly, an inhibitory compound reduces the potential developmental rate ($PDR(T)$) response to temperature. The reduction in PDR is proportional to the titre of the compound and its activity level at temperature T (AT). Actual developmental

rate (i.e. the progression toward diapause completion) at any given temperature is a function of the titre of the inhibitory compound, its activity level, and PDR. The inhibitory compound is removed from the system by exposure to low temperature.

The comparison suggests that the inhibitory compound expresses a virtually identical temperature-dependent activity (A(T)) in the two strains. However, its rate of removal is markedly different. The inhibitory compound is removed more quickly in the AGM than in the NAGM in response to low temperature exposure. And at high temperatures, where there is no reduction in inhibitory compound in the NAGM, the compound is still slightly reduced in the AGM. At the low temperatures that would predominate during winter in the majority of the range of both strains, PDR is slightly higher in the AGM than the NAGM.

These differences will result in a more rapid completion of diapause in the AGM than the NAGM. In addition, diapause may be completed by the AGM in locations where winter temperatures are not sufficiently cold, or of sufficient duration to satisfy diapause in the NAGM, leading to an area of potential establishment that is greater for the the AGM than for the NAGM.

References

Gray, D.R. 2004. **The gypsy moth life stage model: landscape-wide estimates of gypsy moth establishement using a multi-generational phenology model.** Ecological Modelling 176: 155-171.

Gray, D.R., J.A. Logan, F.W. Ravlin, and J.A. Carlson. 1991. **Toward a model of gypsy moth egg phenology: using respiration rates of individual**

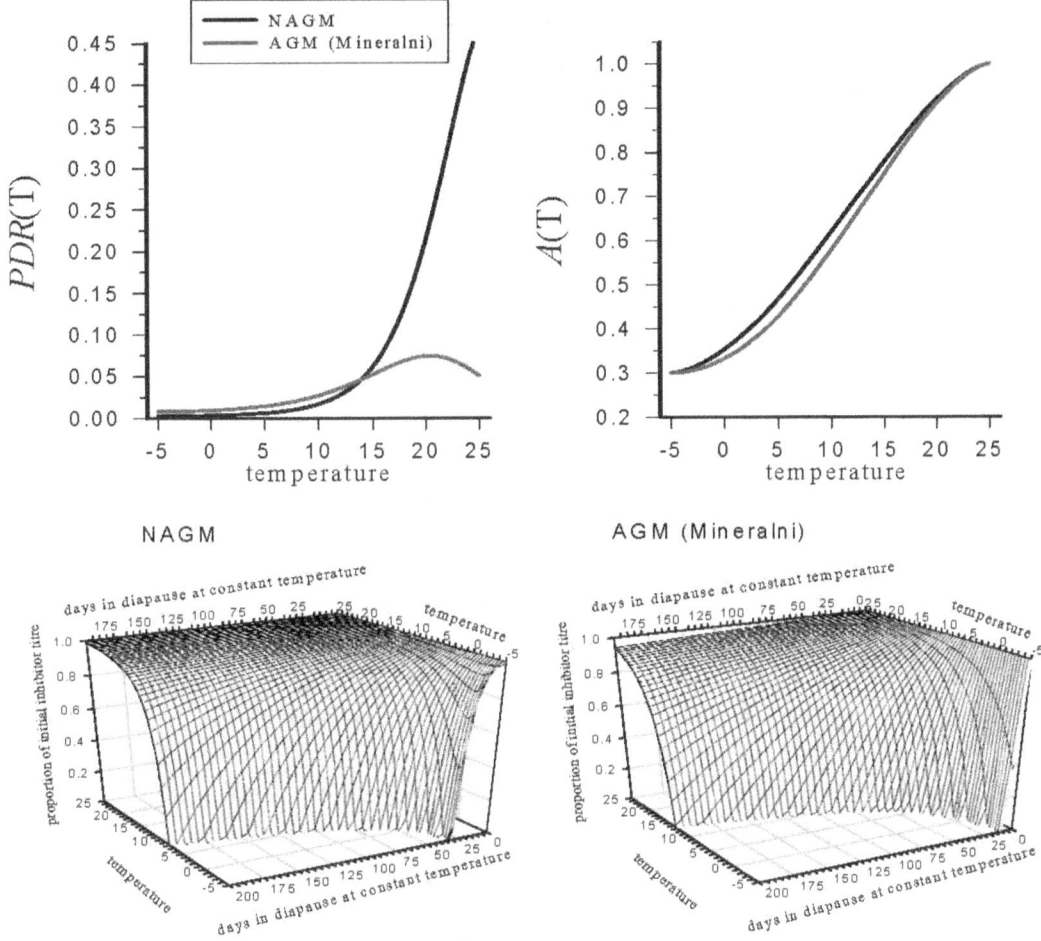

Figure 2.—Illustrates the differences between the NAGM and the AGM in the functional relationships governing diapause development. All temperatures in °C.

eggs to determine temperature-time requirements of prediapause development. Environmental Entomology 20: 1645-1652.

Gray, D.R., F.W. Ravlin, and J.A. Braine. 2001. **Diapause in the gypsy moth: a model of inhibition and development.** Journal of Insect Physiology 47: 173-184.

Gray, D.R., F.W. Ravlin, J. Régnière, and J.A. Logan. 1995. **Further advances toward a model of gypsy moth (*Lymantria dispar* (L.)) egg phenology: respiration rates and thermal responsiveness during diapause, and age-dependent developmental rates in postdiapause.** Journal of Insect Physiology 41: 247-256.

Keena, M.A. 1996. **Comparison of the hatch of *Lymantria dispar* (Lepidoptera: Lymantriidae) eggs from Russia and the United States after exposure to different temperatures and durations of low temperature.** Annals of the Entomological Society of America 89: 564-572.

Leith, H. 1974. **Phenology and seasonality modeling.** Springer-Verlag, Berlin.

Leonard, D.E. 1968. **Diapause in the gypsy moth.** Journal of Economic Entomology 61: 596-598.

Liebhold, A., V. Mastro, and P. Schaefer. 1989. **Learning from the legacy of Leopold Trouvelot.** Bulletin of the Entomological Society of America: 20-22.

HYPERSPECTRAL REMOTE SENSING AND ITS APPLICATIONS

Sarah M. Green and Jason A. Cole

Helicopter Applicators Inc., 1670 York Road, Gettysburg, PA 17325

Abstract

Hemlock woolly adelgid and other forest pests, including invasives species, are a problem for our forests and ecosystems. Surveying and monitoring these problems are done at great cost in both money and time. With the use of hyperspectral remote sensing, vegetation identification and vegetation stress can be analyzed remotely, saving time and surveying a larger area. Hyperspectral Remote Sensing is the process of gathering spectral signatures remotely. Everything has its own signature, similar to that of a fingerprint, making each unique. Helicopter Applicators Incorporated utilizes an AISA Eagle 1K sensor system to gather and analyze these spectral signatures.

Helicopter Applicators Incorporated (HAI) was established in 1974 as an aerial application company, and has since branched into the field of remote sensing. HAI now utilizes a radiometric infrared camera, three-chip digital daytime camera, and hyperspectral sensor system. These systems are mounted on helicopters in gyro-stabilized turrets. The AISA Eagle 1K has a wider swath ability which allows it to be flown higher and therefore gather more data in less time, while at the same or better resolution than other sensors. With customized hardware and software, HAI offers a full end product.

To demonstrate this, Helicopter Applicators was involved with two vegetation management projects in 2004. To perform a mission such as this, HAI is provided a GIS-ready shapefile which is used for data acquisition. The data-cubes are then calibrated and corrected to produce reflectance files. These files are then analyzed spectrally to produce results identifying species and/or stress levels, based upon ground truth spectra or coordinates previously gathered. The images are then geo-rectified and made into GIS-ready files. The species or stress levels are also made into GIS vectors individually so that results can be evaluated from flight to flight, comparable from year to year.

HAI flew 400 linear miles in the Kiski-Conemaugh Watershed for invasives identification. West Virginia University gathered spectra via a handheld spectrometer. The mission was to search for 13 invasives species and then compare results to volunteer data throughout the watershed. HAI conclusively located mile-a-minute, tree of heaven, garlic mustard, purple loosestrife, Norway maple, and phragmites. The second mission was in the Catskill Mountains in New York in cooperation with The University of New Hampshire. HAI flew two polygons to determine hemlock locations and hemlock health, based on GPS ground truth by UNH. Results are still pending but preliminary results are encouraging with both classification and health distributions being qualitatively appropriate. Despite the lack of conclusive results from these two missions, both have shown that hyperspectral imaging will be valuable for detection and delineation, especially with the bands and flexibility of this sensor flown by Helicopter Applicators Inc.

GENETICS AND BIOCHEMICAL VARIATION OF U.S. *AILANTHUS ALTISSIMA* POPULATIONS: A PRELIMINARY DISUCUSSION OF A RESEARCH PLAN

Gary Greer[1] and Preston R. Aldrich[2]

[1]Biology Department, Grand Valley State University, 228 Henry Hall, 1 Campus Drive, Allendale, MI, 49401
[2]Department of Biological Sciences, Benedictine University, Birck Hall 328, 5700 College Road, Lisle, IL 60532-0900

Abstract

Ailanthus altissima (tree-of-heaven, TOH) is an increasing component of NE forests. A member of the tropical family Simaroubaceae, TOH was first imported from China in the late 1700s and has since expanded to most of the lower 48 states (Hu 1979). Although TOH is considered an urban weed, it is appearing with increasing frequency in native forests where it may interfere with native tree regeneration. Greer has documented TOH in small and large gaps and along service roads and skid rows in a near urban forest (Kanawha State Forest) in West Virginia; the largest individuals occurring in closed canopy in skid rows. Several important timber tree species (e.g., oaks and walnut) also favor disturbed habitats, or rely on some form of disturbance to complete their life cycle. Thus, TOH may compete for similar regeneration spaces in forests that are highly fragmented, especially those located near populated areas. Oaks already suffer from regeneration failure in forests that have a suppressed disturbance regime (Parker et al. 1985, Aldrich et al. submitted). As TOH continues to invade North American forests (Huebner 2003), there are reasons to anticipate increasingly detrimental effects on native forests and commercially important timber species.

The novel chemistry of TOH is thought to contribute to its invasiveness. Published research indicates a toxic effect against other plants (allelopathy), rodents, and microbes, all of which could impact forest regeneration (Heisey 1990, 1996). Published works suggest that quassinoid triterpenes, primarily ailanthone, are responsible for much of the toxicity of this species (Kubota et al. 1996, De Feo et al. 2003, Okunade et al. 2003). A study by Greer and colleagues found reduced understory biodiversity beneath TOH canopies compared to native canopies. A series of germination experiments by Greer demonstrated that TOH toxicity, in leaves and surrounding soil, is greater on a per gram basis in juveniles (2 yrs old or less) than in older age-classes and that minor injury to TOH induces an increase in phytotoxin production.

Little is known about naturalized genetic or biochemical variation in U.S. populations of TOH (Feret 1985, Feret and Bryant 1974, Feret et al. 1974). There has been considerable pharmaceutical prospecting in *Ailanthus* in search of cures for AIDS, cancer, and a variety of other ailments (Ogura et al. 1997, Chang and Woo 2003). Despite the attention given to *A. altissima* and ailanthone, there are no studies that have attempted to document regional variation in ailanthone. Many invasive plants experience an "ecological release" upon entering new habitat because their natural enemy herbivores are left behind. If the post-introduction range expansion has been rapid, as appears to be the case, the species may be lacking in genetic and biochemical variation, especially if the introductions involved relatively few founding events. Moreover, reductions in herbivore pressures might relax the production of a metabolically costly toxin, yielding uniformly low levels of ailanthone outside of China. Alternatively, *A. altissima* may be both genetically and biochemically variable. The species is a polyploidy with 2N=80 and changes in chromosome number may be fueling an adaptive radiation into its new habitat. Adaptations to local environments might involve development of ecotypes that vary in toxicity and invasiveness. Genetic variation in TOH might differ significantly between Eastern and Western sides of the continental divide. TOH colonization of the Eastern U.S. may have resulted from very few, perhaps only one, founding event. If so, much of TOH's genetic variation may have been purged, producing a problematic though genetically benign species in the Eastern U.S. Alternatively, many founding events are believed to have occurred in the Western U.S. from Chinese immigrants, establishing populations with greater genetic diversity.

We are collecting seeds from 10-12 sites across the U.S. along an East-West transect, with focused sampling from WV and the midwest. We will use molecular genetic methods to characterize patterns of diversity in the chloroplast genome, and cytogenetic methods to characterize karyotypic variation in the nuclear genome across the range. We also will quantify variation in levels of toxic compounds through chemical assays and bioassays on plants, microbes and rodents. Some rodent species are known to eat TOH whereas others avoid it (Ostfeld et al. 1997), and such a difference might influence patterns of seedling establishment in forests.

Our research should prove useful as a foundation in basic TOH biology that may aid efforts to manage and control its spread. Knowledge of the underlying patterns of variation will allow identification of diversity hotspots that could be targeted for elimination. Patterns of genetic variation also can be used to evaluate past episodes of migration and future threats of spread and gene pool change.

References

Aldrich P.R., G.R. Parker, J. Romero-Severson, and C.H. Michler (submitted) **Confirmation of oak recruitment failure in Indiana old-growth forest: 75 years of data.** Forest Science.

Chang, Y.-S., and E.-R. Woo. 2003. **Korean medicinal plants inhibiting to human immunodeficiency virus type 1 (HIV-1) fusion.** Phytotherapy Research 17: 426-429.

De Feo, V.L. De Martino, E. Quaranta, and C. Pizza. 2003. **Isolation of phytotoxic compounds from Tree-of-Heaven (*Ailanthus altissima* Swingle).** Journal of Agricultural and Food Chemistry 51: 1177-1180.

Feret, P.P. 1985. *Ailanthus*: variation, cultivation, and frustration. Journal of Arboriculture 11: 361-368.

Feret, P.P. and R.L. Bryant. 1974. **Genetic differences between American and Chinese *Ailanthus* seedlings.** Silvae Genetica 23: 144-148.

Feret, P.P., R.L. Bryant, and J.A. Ramsey. 1974. **Genetic variation among American seed sources of *Ailanthus altissima* (Mill.) Swingle.** Scientia Horticulturae 2: 405-411.

Heisey, R.M. 1990. **Allelopathic and herbicidal effects of extracts from tree of heaven (*Ailanthus altissima*).** American Journal of Botany 77: 662-670.

Heisey, R.M. 1996. **Identification of an allelopathic compound from *Ailanthus altissima* (Simaroubaceae) and characterization of its herbicidal activity.** American Journal of Botany 83:192-200.

Huebner, C.D. 2003. **Vulnerability of oak-dominated forests in West Virginia to invasive plants: temporal and spatial patterns of nine exotic species using herbarium records and land classification data.** Castanea 68:1-14.

Hu, S.Y. 1979. *Ailanthus.* Arnoldia 39: 29-50.

Kubota, K. et al. 1996. **Two new quassinoids, Ailanthinols A and B, and related compounds from *Ailanthus altissima.*** Journal of Natural Products 59: 683-686.

Ogura, M., G.A. Cordell, A.D. Kinghorn, and N.R. Farnsworth. 1997. **Potential anticancer agents VI. Constituents of *Ailanthus excelsa* (Simaroubaceae).** Llyodia 40: 579-584.

Okunade, A.L. et al. 2003. **Antiplasmodial activity of extracts and quassinoids isolated from seedlings of *Ailanthus altissima* (Simaroubaceae).** Phytotherapy Research 17: 675-677.

Ostfeld, R.S., R.H. Manson, and C.D. Canham. 1997. **Effects of rodents on survival of tree seeds and seedlings invading old fields.** Ecology 78: 1531-1542.

Parker G.R., D.J. Leopold, and J.K. Eichenberger. 1985. **Tree dynamics in an old-growth, deciduous forest.** Forest Ecology and Management 11: 31-57.

A HIGHLY EFFECTIVE TREE INJECTION METHOD USING IMIDACLOPRID FOR THE CONTROL OF EMERALD ASH BORER (*AGRILUS PLANIPENNIS*)

Blair Helson[1], Dean Thompson[1], Nicole McKenzie[2] and Gard Otis[2]

[1]Canadian Forest Service, Natural Resources Canada, Sault Ste Marie, ON, P6A 2E5
[2]Environmental Biology, University of Guelph, Guelph, Ontario, Canada N1G 2W1

Abstract

The objectives of this experiment were to determine the comparative uptake, translocation of imidacloprid and resultant efficacy following early or late season stem injections.

Fifty green ash trees located in a residential area of Windsor, Ontario and ranging from 7 to 26 cm dbh, were injected with an experimental 5% formulation of imidacloprid (ITIS) using Systemic Tree Injection Tubes (STIT) at a dosage of 0.25 g/cm dbh on either 25 June or 17 September 2003. Efficacy was evaluated both in terms of controlling emerald ash borer (EAB) and with respect to protection of high value trees. Approximately 1 year post treatment, comparative assessments of adult emergence, exit holes on branches and trunks, crown die back, foliar density and epicormic shoots were made for both treated and untreated trees on the site. Based on these key response parameters, excellent control of EAB and effective protection of the injected trees was observed 1 year following early season injections. Although the late season injections appeared to provide less control of EAB, protection from crown dieback was good.

Quantitative analysis of imidacloprid concentrations in critical foliar and stem tissues upon which adult and larval life stages of EAB feed respectively confirmed that uptake and translocation of imidacloprid was rapid resulting in exposure concentrations well in excess of toxicity thresholds for both adults and larvae within 7 days of treatment. Following early season treatments, imidacloprid concentrations remained above toxicity threshold levels throughout the 83-day sampling period. Foliar concentrations observed in the spring following late-season treatments were comparatively lower but still well in excess of toxicity thresholds for EAB adults.

UPDATE ON SURVEY AND ERADICATION OF THE BROWN SPRUCE LONGHORN BEETLE, AND SUMMARY OF RECENT RESEARCH

Gord Henry[1], Jon Sweeney[2], Wayne MacKay,[2] Richard Hamelin[3], Georgette Smith[2],
Marie-José Côté[4] and Nicole Lecours[3]

[1]Canadian Food Inspection Agency, 59 Camelot Drive, Ottawa, ON K1A 0Y9
[2]Natural Resources Canada, Canadian Forest Service - Atlantic Forestry Centre, PO Box 4000, Fredericton NB, E3B 5P7
[3]Natural Resources Canada, Canadian Forest Service - Laurentian Forestry Centre, 1055 Rue due P.E.P.S., Sainte-Foy, QC, G1V 4C7
[4]Canadian Food Inspection Agency, 3851 Fallowfield road, Ottawa, ON, K2H 8P9

Abstract

In 2000, the Canadian Food Inspection Agency (CFIA) initiated a science-based eradication program to eliminate the brown spruce longhorn beetle (BSLB) in Halifax, Nova Scotia, Canada. The BSLB is an introduced alien invasive species, native to Europe, that could threaten the health of spruce forests and urban trees in impacted areas. The BSLB program focuses on public awareness, surveillance, research, quarantine control measures, certification protocols, and pest mitigation activates. Currently, the only effective detection tool is visual inspection, and the most effective control tool is the removal and destruction of host trees. To date, the CFIA has removed over 6300 spruce trees, with approximately 300 removed during 2004. Program results appear promising, as the number of positive trees detected has decreased dramatically since 2000. Hurricane Juan caused substantial blowdown of trees in Halifax and other parts of Nova Scotia on 28 September 2003. Because the BSLB breeds in windfall and fresh logs, as well as live spruce, there were concerns that populations might build in windfall that was not salvaged before adult emergence in the summer of 2005. Large-diameter, green, windfelled spruce trees that displayed no external signs of BSLB were sampled from nine sites, eight within the BSLB quarantine zone and one outside the quarantine zone, in late fall of 2004; they were milled to determine the percentage infested with the BSLB. Eight of nine sites contained infested windfall, with an overall mean of 14% (0-43%) infestation. The heaviest infestation was on McNabs Island, an area so badly damaged by Hurricane Juan that regular surveys to locate and remove infested trees were not possible until the fall of 2004. The eradication program is being reviewed to determine strategies for mitigating the risk of BSLB population increase and spread posed by the large volume of windfelled spruce.

Highlights of some recent research on the biology, survey, and control of the BSLB were presented. Two North American species of parasitic wasps (one braconid, one ichneumonid) that commonly parasitize the native *Tetropium cinnamopterum* have also been recorded for the first time from *T. fuscum* (see Sweeney et al. poster abstract in these Proceedings). With greater knowledge of the factors affecting parasitoid foraging and survival, it may be possible to enhance their impact on the BSLB in Nova Scotia. *Beauveria bassiana* is being tested as means of suppressing BSLB populations, by applying conidospores directly to spruce bait logs or by wrapping conidia-treated polyester bands around the stems of spruce trees (see Sweeney et al. poster abstract). Results indicate that the BSLB is susceptible to *B. bassiana* under field conditions and that tree bands may be a better strategy to pursue than applications to bait logs. Species-specific molecular markers and real-time PCR assays have been developed that demonstrate great promise in rapidly distinguishing *T. fuscum* from nine other *Tetropium* species, as well as other asemine cerambycid out-groups. Further tests are planned to validate the markers and test their efficacy with environmental samples, such as eggs, frass, and exuviae. A large whole-tree drum chipper was tested for its efficacy as a phytosanitary tool for the treatment of BSLB-infested logs in March 2004. No *Tetropium* spp. adults or similar size insects (e.g., wood wasps, parasitoids, other cerambycids) emerged from chips compared with significant numbers that emerged from logs. Some very small scolytid beetles and flies (1-3 mm) survived to emerge from chips, suggesting that small life stages of BSLB (e.g., eggs, 1st or 2nd instars) might survive but very few chips (≤ 0.25%) had intact bark and sufficient size for successful development of *T. fuscum*. The results indicate that chips had negligible phytosanitary risk and that chipping was a suitable treatment for BSLB infested material. The CFIA has approved phytosanitary wood chipping protocols that will help landowners clear windfall from properties and mitigate the spread of BSLB.

SURVEY AND EVALUATION OF POTENTIAL NATURAL ENEMIES OF ANOPLOPHORA GLABRIPENNIS AND A. CHINENSIS

Franck Hérard[1], Marie-Claude Bon[1], Matteo Maspero[2], Christian Cocquempot[3] and Jaime Lopez[1]

[1]European Biological Control Laboratory, USDA-ARS, Montferrier-sur-Lez, France
[2]Fondazione Minoprio, Como, Italy
[3]INRA, Montpellier, France

Abstract

A survey was attempted to find possible new associations between introduced *Anoplophora* spp. and natural enemies from the European fauna. We report here the first results of this survey and of the evaluation of these potential natural enemies based on both field and laboratory tests.

1. Natural enemies of *Anoplophora chinensis* in Italy:

For the first time in early 2002, at Parabiago, we found a gregarious egg parasitoid of CLB as hibernating larvae in unhatched host eggs. The new species was described by Delvare et al. (2005) as *Aprostocetus anoplophorae* n. sp. (Hym: Eulophidae).

1.1. *Aprostocetus anoplophorae* n. sp. (Hym.: Eulophidae):

At Parabiago, Italy, we determined that the parasitoid activity begins in late June - early July, and both phenologies of the host and of the parasitoid are closely synchronized. Sentinel host plants infested with CLB eggs were attractive for *A. anoplophorae* whereas those infested with ALB eggs were not. However, one ALB egg was found to be attacked by a Chalcid. Molecular methods were used to help in identifying the female specimen found in the ALB egg. Results showed that the female specimen could be assigned to the species *A. anoplophorae*. More field and laboratory tests would be required to precise the degree of specificity of *A. anoplophorae* towards CLB and ALB, and to determine to what extent the susceptibility of ALB to it can be enhanced.

1. 2. *Spathius erythrocephalus* Wesmael (Hym.: Braconidae):

In early July 2004, in the field, at Parabiago, 7 newly hatched CLB larvae in a sentinel host plant (*Acer negundo*), were attacked by *S. erythrocephalus*. In the laboratory, fertilized *S. erythrocephalus* females aged 5 to 42 days old were able to successfully attack both ALB and CLB hosts. At 22 °C, their progeny in *Anoplophora* hosts developed (from egg laying through adult emergence) in 30 days. Longevity of *S. erythrocephalus* females and males was 48.7 ± 4.8 days, and 42 days, respectively. The ability of *S. erythrocephalus* females to detect and to attack very early stages of the targets is noteworthy. Further evaluation of the new associations *S. erythrocephalus* - *Anoplophora* spp. is being considered.

2. *Sclerodermus* spp. (Hym.: Bethylidae):

In the laboratory, host acceptance and host suitability were studied by rearing *Sclerodermus abdominalis* (SA), *Sclerodermus* sp. SC1, and Sclerodermus sp. SC4 on various host species, in small plastic containers. *S. abdominalis* paralyzed and parasitized small hosts as *P. rufipes* and *P. testaceus*, and small larvae of ALB as well, but it was less effective in neutralizing big larvae of ALB. More successful attacks of big ALB larvae were performed by groups of *Sclerodermus* females. A study of the search rate of a host by SC1 and SC4, using living rooted cuttings of *Salix* sp. inoculated with big larvae of *Lamia textor* (Col.: Cerambycidae) showed that SC4 females performed better than SC1 females in reaching and paralyzing a host. However, in the wet galleries bored under the bark of living plants the preservation of the attacked hosts was poor. The species of *Sclerodermus* tested may be more effective against cerambycids attacking dying or dead trees or branches where they find a dry habitat. However, more tests on the search rate of SC1 and SC4 are being planned using young larvae of ALB in living plants.

References

Delvare, G., M.-C. Bon, F. Hérard, C. Cocquempot, M. Maspero, and M. Colombo. 2004. **Description of Aprostocetus anoplophorae sp. n. (Hymenoptera, Eulophidae), a new egg parasitoid of the invasive pest Anoplophora chinensis (Förster) (Coleoptera, Cerambycidae).** Ann. Soc. Entomol. Fr., 40 (3-4): in press.

ANOPLOPHORA IN EUROPE: INFESTATIONS AND MANAGEMENT RESPONSES

Franck Hérard[1], Hannes Krehan[2], Ullrich Benker[3], Carolin Boegel[3], Reiner Schrage[4], Ellena Chauvat[5], Mariangela Ciampitti[6], Matteo Maspero[7] and Piotr Bialooki[8]

[1]European Biological Control Laboratory, USDA-ARS, Montpellier, France
[2]Austrian Federal Office and Research Centre for Forests, Vienna, Austria
[3]Bavarian State Research Center for Agriculture, Freising, Germany
[4]North Rhine-Westphalian Plant Protection service, Bonn, Germany
[5]French Plant Protection service, Paris, France
[6]Lombardy Plant Protection service, Milan, Italy
[7]Minoprio Foundation, Como, Italy
[8]Polish Plant Protection service, Gdansk, Poland

Abstract

Anoplophora glabripennis (ALB)

At the end of 2004 four sites of infestation by ALB have been detected in three countries of Europe: Austria in 2001, at Braunau am Inn (Upper Austria); France in 2003, at Gien (Loiret), and in 2004 at Sainte-Anne-sur-Brivet (Loire Atlantique); and Germany in 2004, at Neukirchen am Inn (Bavaria). So far, all infestations are located in urban environments.

Circumstances of the ALB discoveries

At Braunau (Austria), symptoms of unidentified attacks were first observed in November 2000 by employees of the municipal gardening office on trees near a site where wood packing material, which was used for the importation of stones and cast-iron from China, was stored. In July 2001, ALB adults were collected on the damaged trees. The Austrian Federal Office and Research Centre for Forests in Vienna identified the insects, started monitoring the pest at Braunau, and sent alerts in Austria to the regional plant protection services. As Braunau is right next to the Austrian-German boarder, alerts were also sent in Germany to the Bavarian plant protection service.

At Neukirchen (Germany), symptoms of decline were observed on branches of maple trees around a cemetery opposite a building belonging to a company storing granite stones imported from China. Since 2001 in this area, all companies importing goods from Eastern Asia were alerted to the risks of introduction of exotic pests. The Bavarian plant protection service sampled larvae from the damaged trees and passed them to the Austrian Federal Office and Research Centre for Forests in Vienna for DNA analyzes. Results showed that the larval specimens could be assigned to the species *A. glabripennis*. The Bavarian plant protection service started monitoring the pest in Neukirchen.

In 2002, at Gien (France), during a barbecue party that took place at the end of the school year, three longhorned beetles were disturbed by smoke and fell down on a table placed under the crown of a maple tree. The unknown specimens were placed by a student in a container for later identification. As the specimens did not belong to a species from the French fauna, in March 2003, they were passed to an entomologist in the Museum of Natural History in Dijon. The person, realizing that the insect may belong to a dangerous exotic pest, passed the specimens to the National Laboratory of the French plant protection service (LNPV) in Montpellier where they were identified as ALB. In April 2003, the regional plant protection service in Orléans was alerted, and a monitoring of the pest was begun at Gien. Larvae were sampled and submitted for DNA analyzes to EBCL, Montpellier. The ongoing infestation by ALB in several trees in Gien was confirmed.

At Sainte-Anne-sur-Brivet (France), in July 2004, an adult beetle was collected on a willow in a private yard near a square recently paved with granite stones imported from China. The person brought the beetle to the city hall which then sent it on July 15, 2004, to the LNPV in Montpellier where it was identified as ALB. In early August 2004 the alerted regional plant protection service in Nantes started monitoring the pest on susceptible trees in, and around the village. Oaks were also monitored because an ALB adult was observed roaming about on an oak adjacent to ALB-infested maples; moreover, a few big

Table 1.—Results of monitoring of the *Anoplophora* spp. infestations in Europe

Pest	Site	2001	2002	2003	2004	TOTAL
ALB	Braunau Am Inn (Austria)	38 (89)	22 (0)	8 (25)	27 (4)	95 (118)
ALB	Neukirchen Am Inn (Germany)				16 (13)	16 (13)
	Gien (France)			30 (0)	12 (12)	42 (12)
ALB	Sainte-Anne -Sur -Brivet (France)				55 (?)	55 (?)
CLB	Soyons (France)			2 (3)	0 (0)	2 (3)
CLB	Parabiago (Italy)	? (?)	18 (?)	27 (?)	741* (?)	786 (?)

Values are numbers of *Anoplophora* spp.-infested trees (values in parentheses are numbers of adult beetles collected).
*Out of 741 infested trees, only 30 trees were fully destroyed at Parabiago.

exit holes of an unknown (at that time) insect were seen on some *Quercus pedunculata* and *Quercus americana* near the ALB-infested maples.

History of the ALB discoveries and management responses

In 2002, the commission of the European communities issued the directive 2002/36/EC notifying the member states of the necessity to take measures to protect the community against *A. glabripennis*.

In the 4 ALB-infested sites, given the number of pest damages and exit holes on some particular trees, it is thought that the initial infestation occurred at least 5 years before the pest discovery. In Austria and Germany, a decree on the ALB control was issued immediately after the pest discovery, and eradication started without delay. At Gien, because of the particular circumstances of the pest discovery, a year elapsed before a decree on its control was issued and eradication started. At Sainte-Anne-sur-Brivet, 2 months elapsed before eradication started, but in the meantime the infested trees were sprayed twice with a contact insecticide (bifenthrin) to kill the ALB adults emerging during summer 2004. In the 4 sites, ALB was introduced as larvae and/or pupae in tunnels in fresh untreated wood packing material imported from China. In the four sites, special efforts were made to increase public awareness. In France,

information about the ALB problem was also spread through the association of the mayors of France. In the four sites, the monitoring of the ALB infestations was made by visual examination of susceptible trees, using binoculars, ladders, bucket trucks, and tree climbers. Depending on the site, 2 to 10 people working 1 to 3 days a week were involved in the monitoring. In each site, a 1-km radius around each infested tree was examined. A 1 or 2 km- width buffer zone was delimited around each infested area. Near Braunau, the buffer zone was extended to the whole political district. In Austria, France and Germany, the monitoring concerned the public area, and the private yards as well. It was extended outside the infested areas, around some importers of goods from eastern Asia, and in Austria, around some importers of goods from the USA. The infested areas were quarantined by banning any movement of living susceptible plants, or firewood. In each of the four infested sites several local partners were involved in the monitoring and in the eradication of the pest. Funding to cover the cost of monitoring and eradication was primarily supplied by the regional administrations.

Fate of the ALB infestations in Europe

The results of the monitoring in the four ALB-infested sites are shown in Table 1. Each year, in all sites, fairly low numbers of infested trees were found. In Braunau

Table 2—Host plants of *Anoplophora glabripennis* in Europe, at the end of 2004

Species		Braunau Am Inn (Austria)	Neukirchen Am Inn (Germany)	Gien (France)	Sainte-Anne-Sur-Brivet (France)
Maple trees	*Acer* spp.		✓ (5)	✓ (31)	✓ (23)
Boxelder	*Acer negundo*			✓	✓
Silver maple	*Acer saccharinum*	✓		✓	✓
Norway maple	*Acer platanoides*	✓		✓	✓
Sycamore	*Acer pseudoplatanus*	✓			
Plane tree	*Platanus* sp.	✓			
Beech	*Fagus sylvatica* "atropunicea"	✓			
Beech	*Fagus sylvatica* "asplenifolia"	✓			
Birch	*Betula* sp.	✓	✓ (2)	✓ (8)	✓ (23)
Horse chesnut	*Aesculus hippocastanum*	✓	✓ (4)	✓ (1)	✓ (3)
Poplar	*Populus* sp.		✓ (1)		✓ (1)
Willow	*Salix* sp.		✓ (4)	✓ (2)	✓ (4)
Plum tree	*Prunus* sp.				✓ (1)
	Total	95	16	42	55

Values are numbers of infested trees in each species

where the first infestation was discovered 4 years ago, the number of infested trees newly detected during 2004 was not much lower than in 2001; however, no ALB infested tree was found outside the city. The infested trees were distributed at Braunau in a 0.5 km radius, at Neukirchen in a 0.2 km radius, at Gien in a 0.5 km radius, and at Sainte-Anne-sur-Brivet in a 0.2 km radius. In the four sites all the infested trees were cut, the stumps were uprooted, and all plant material was incinerated. At Braunau and at Neukirchen, the infested plant material was first chipped then burnt. The host plants of ALB in Europe at the end of 2004 are listed in Table 2. Maple trees were the preferred host plants in most sites. At Sainte-Anne-sur-Brivet, birches were also much affected. In this site, 17 *Quercus rubra* and five *Quercus robur*, which were located near ALB-infested maples bore exit holes of an unknown wood borer and were also destroyed. Dissection of infested logs of the oaks showed that *Cerambyx cerdo*, the Great capricorn beetle, native to Europe, was one of the pests present in the oaks. DNA analyzes of samples of cerambycid larvae from the oaks by M.-C. Bon, EBCL, Montpellier, showed two different non-ALB profiles.

Anoplophora chinensis (CLB)

A. chinensis females lay most of their eggs around the collar of trees. The larvae develop downwards and many of them tunnel their way in roots. Ninety percent of the CLB population is below ground level. The range of host plants seems even wider in CLB than in ALB. At the end of 2004, two sites of infestation by CLB have been detected in two countries of Europe: Italy in 2000, at Parabiago, and France in 2003, at Soyons.

Circumstances of the CLB discoveries

At Soyons (France), in 2002, an adult beetle emerged from a bonsai, at the client's residence. On June 18, 2003, the dead insect was sent to the LNPV, Montpellier, where it was identified as CLB. On June 18, 2003, the source nursery was visited and five free CLB adults and 11 fresh exit holes were found on two big Norwegian maple trees adjacent to the nursery building. The LNPV confirmed that the collected specimens were all CLBs. At Soyons, the Rhône-Alpes plant protection service started monitoring the pest on susceptible trees around the nursery of bonsais.

At Parabiago (Italy), in 2000, the first discovery of CLB occurred during a survey program carried out by the Institute of Entomology, Agricultural University of Milan (IE-AUM), with financial support of the Lombardy Plant Protection Service (LPPS). The purpose of the monitoring was to check possible new introductions of exotic pests in nurseries and greenhouses near Milan. The first adult of CLB was collected by a technician in one of the nurseries. CLB was introduced as eggs, larvae and/or pupae in living host plants (bonsais) imported from the Far East. The insect was identified on June 8, 2000, by the IE-AUM, in collaboration with the Museum of Natural History of Milan. Another specimen of the same species was found again among dried insects in a collection box that was made in 1997 at Parabiago. The CLB discovery was reported by Colombo & Limonta (2001). In 2002, a first monitoring program was implemented by the IE-AUM, with the collaboration of the Minoprio Foundation, and financial support from the LPPS.

History of the CLB discoveries and management responses

Because of the repeated interceptions of exotic pests including *Anoplophora* sp. at ports of entry, in 2000, the commission of the European communities issued the directive 2000/29/EC notifying the member states of a list of harmful organisms, including *A. chinensis*, whose introduction into and spread within all member states are banned.

At Soyons, it is thought that the initial CLB infestation occurred at least 5 years before the pest discovery. CLB was introduced as eggs, larvae and/or pupae in living host plants (bonsais) imported from the Far East. Because of the late identification of the first CLB adult found, 1 year elapsed before a decree on CLB control was issued and eradication started. The monitoring was made by visual examination of the base of the susceptible trees. Two people working 1 day a week were involved in the monitoring. A 1-km radius around the infested trees was examined and a 1 km- width buffer zone was delimited around the infested area. The monitoring concerned the public area, and the private yards as well. The infested area was quarantined as for any movement of living susceptible plants, or firewood.

At Parabiago, a collection box of dried insects, made around 1982, and containing CLB specimens was found again recently, which could mean that the very first CLB introduction may have occurred in Italy, about 20 years ago, and not 5 years before Colombo & Limonta's

report (2001). Since this report, 4 years elapsed before a decree on CLB control was issued and eradication started. The decree, published in Bollettino Ufficiale della Regione Lombardia, Serie Ordinaria N. 6 - 2 Febbraio 2004; D.d.g. 26 Gennaio 2004 n°. 731, stipulates that 3 control measures may be used:

1. The CLB infested trees must be cut and the plant parts (including the stump with the roots) removed and destroyed

2. If stump uprooting is difficult, the stump must be killed with herbicides, and covered with wire mesh screen on an area matching the projection on soil of the tree crown

3. On big valuable trees, the LPPS may decide that the trees won't be destroyed if the infestation is low. In this case, a sleeve cage of wire mesh screen is placed around the base of the trunks, and a sheet of wire mesh screen on ground, as well. The wire mesh screens are supposed to contain the CLB populations.

During 2004, special efforts of information were made to increase public awareness. The monitoring was made by visual examination of the base of the susceptible trees. Four to eight people working 1 day a week were involved in the monitoring. A 1-km radius around the infested trees was examined and a 1 km- width buffer zone was delimited around the infested area. At Parabiago, so far, the monitoring concerned the public area, and a very small number of private yards, on request from the owners, only. Outside the CLB-infested area, nurseries importing bonsais are surveyed twice a year. The infested area was quarantined banning any movement of living susceptible plants, or firewood. In both CLB-infested sites several local partners were involved in the monitoring and in the eradication of the pest. Funding to cover the cost of monitoring and eradication was primarily supplied by the regional administrations.

Fate of the CLB infestations in Europe

The results of the monitoring in both CLB-infested sites are shown in Table 1. At Soyons, 2 infested trees only were detected. They were cut, the stumps were uprooted, and all the plant parts were incinerated. At

Table 3—Host plants of *Anoplophora chinensis* in Europe, at the end of 2004

Species		Soyons (France)	Parabiago (Italy)
Maple	*Acer sp.*		✓
Boxelder	*Acer negundo*		✓
Siver maple	*Acer saccharinum*		✓
Norway maple	*Acer platanoides*	✓	✓
Sycamore	*Acer pseudoplatanus*		✓
European hornbeam	*Carpinus betulus*		✓
Hazel	*Corylus* sp.		✓
Plane tree	*Platanus* sp.		✓
Beech	*Fagus sylvatica*		✓
Crape myrtle	*Lagerstroemia* sp.		✓
Apple tree	*Malus sp.*		✓
Birch tree	*Betula sp.*		✓
Birch tree	*Betula alba*		✓
Silver birch	*Betula pendula*		✓
Horse chesnut	*Aesculus hippocastanum*		✓
Poplar	*Populus sp.*		✓
Lombardy poplar	*Populus nigra*		✓
Cherry laurel	*Prunus laurocerasus*		✓
Rose	*Rosa*		✓
Elm	*Ulmus* sp.		✓
European cotoneaster	*Cotoneaster* sp.		✓
Common oak	*Quercus robur*		✓
Hawthorn	*Crataegus*		✓
	Total	2	786

Parabiago, more CLB-infested trees were found each year at an increasing distance from the nursery of bonsais where the infestation started. In 2003, not only big trees but even shrubs like the Cherry laurels, *Prunus laurocerasus*, which are widely used to make hedges around private yards were attacked by CLB. During 2004, the CLB population exploded. Even old roses in flower beds separating roadways of some large streets were found attacked by CLB. During the summer 2004, an intensified monitoring by the LPPS allowed to detect 741 infested trees spread in 13 municipalities. The infested area covers 57 km² inside a 15 km radius. All infested sites are included in a polygon delimited by the four cities Gallarate, Inveruno, Pogliano Milanese, and Saronno. At the present time, out of the 741 infested trees detected, only 30 trees were fully destroyed, 348 trees were cut and the stump treated with herbicides and covered with wire mesh screen, and 363 trees were not cut, but their base of trunk was wrapped in a sleeve cage of wire mesh screen, according to the directions of the LPPS. The host plants of CLB in Europe at the end of 2004 are listed in Table 3.

Recent Interceptions

In 2004, at Mönchengladbach (Germany) one ALB adult was intercepted on *Acer palmatum* in a private yard. Despite of a very intensive monitoring, no infested tree and no other ALB adult was found. No possible source of infestation was identified. In 2004, at Gdynia (Poland) one free adult of ALB (or CLB - unclear, yet) was found at a florist's shop on *Acer palmatum*. This would be the first report of ALB from a bonsai, outside its native area.

Discussion

In all sites except at Parabiago, the infestations seem to have been detected before the numbers of infested trees is high, and before the pests leave the urban habitats. Proper monitoring and eradication measures were applied, and the *Anoplophora* are in course of eradication in most sites. In contrast, the presence of CLB in Italy may be irreversible, already. The monitoring efforts should take into account the private properties, systematically; so far, only the voluntary requests from private owners were considered. Even though the eradication of CLB seems difficult, a much more aggressive campaign of destruction of the infested trees should be conducted very quickly to limit the spread of the pest.

References

Colombo, M. and Limonta, L. 2001. *Anoplophora malasiaca* **Thomson (Coleoptera, Cerambycidae, Lamiinae, Lamiini) in Europe.** Bollettino di Zoologia Agraria e di Bachicoltura 33, 65-68.

QUANTIFYING TRANSMISSION OF MICROSPORIDIA IN THE FIELD

Gernot Hoch[1], Vincent D'Amico[2], Leellen F. Solter[3], Michael L. McManus[4], and Milan Zubrik[5]

[1]BOKU - Univ. of Nat. Res. and Appl. Life Sci., Hasenauerstr. 38, 1190 Vienna, Austria
[2]USDA FS - Northeastern Research Station/University of Delaware, Townsend Hall, Newark, DE 19716
[3]Illinois Natural History Survey, 607 E. Peabody Dr., Champaign, IL 61820
[4]USDA FS - Northeastern Research Station, 51 Millpond Rd., Hamden, CT 06514
[5]Forest Research Institute, Lesnicka 11, 96923 Banska Stiavnica, Slovak Republic

Abstract

Microsporidia transmission in terrestrial insect populations is still not well understood. In our study, we attempted to quantify transmission of one microsporidium in forest lepidopteran larvae; as far as we are aware this is the first time such an experiment has been performed under semi-field conditions. We used a naturally occurring *Nosema* sp. that was isolated from a *L. dispar* population near Levishte, Bulgaria. The parasite propagates in the silk glands, fat body and Malpighian tubules of the host. Infective spores are released into the environment from living larvae, most likely via silk and faeces as well as from cadavers.

Field cages (1x1x2 m) were installed around each of 15 *Quercus petraea* trees of 2 m height and with similar foliage density on a young oak plantation. *Nosema*-infected and uninfected *L. dispar* larvae (hereafter referred to as initially-infected and test larvae) were placed into the cages. Numbers of initially-infected and test larvae per cage were 10:90, 20:80, 30:70, 40:60, 50:50; each treatment ratio was replicated in three cages. Larvae were removed after 21 d of exposure. Larvae were reared individually in the laboratory for an additional 11 d, then diagnosed for microsporidian infections using phase contrast microscopy. We succeeded in recovering approximately 70% of the exposed larvae in each cage after 21 d. Ratios of recovered initially-infected and test larvae remained consistent with the ratios released. Upon dissection many test larvae were determined to be infected, proving that transmission had occurred under the experimental semi-field conditions. At the lower infection ratios, the numbers of *Nosema*-positive test larvae followed the expected pattern, considering the number of initially-infected larvae in each cage. However, at higher densities, percent infection in the cages appeared to level off. Mean infection percentages (± SE) in test insects were 19.1±5.2 at 10:90 initially-infected larvae to test larvae, 26.5±0.3 at 20:80, 38.9±7.7 at 30:70, 28.3±11.4 at 40:60, and 32.0±4.3 at 50:50. Unfortunately, the scale and time requirements of this experiments limited us to three replicates per treatment and, to a certain degree, inconsistent transmission did not allow us to draw definite conclusions. A repetition of this experiment in Spring 2005 should help to clarify our results.

RANGE EXPANSION OF THE PINE PROCESSIONARY MOTH IN EUROPE II: ACTIVITY AND SURVIVAL OF *THAUMETOPOEA PITYOCAMPA* (LEP.: THAUMETOPOEIDAE) DURING THE WINTER MONTHS IN AN ALPINE VALLEY

Gernot Hoch[1], Sigrid Netherer[1], Josef Pennerstorfer[1], Peter Baier[1], Andrea Battisti[2] and Axel Schopf[1]

[1]BOKU - University of Natural Resources and Applied Life Sciences Vienna, Hasenauerstr. 38, 1190 Wien, Austria
[2]University of Padova, Via Romea 16, 35020 - Legnaro (PD), Italy

Abstract

The larvae of the pine processionary moth, *Thaumetopoea pityocampa* (Den. & Schiff.) (Lep.: Thaumetopoeidae) feed on needles of various pine species and other conifers; in many Mediterranean countries the species has permanent pest status. The socio-economic impact of *T. pityocampa* is of particular importance due to the urticating hairs of the caterpillars that cause severe contact dermatitis in humans and warm-blooded animals. In recent decades, an expansion of the range of *T. pityocampa* has been observed—both, northwards, such as in the Paris Basin in France, and altitudinal, such as in the Venosta valley in northern Italy. Winter temperature may be the thriving force behind range expansion since *T. processionea* hibernates in the larval stage without entering diapause. Larvae live gregariously in conspicuous silk nests that are left during the night for feeding, when conditions are favourable. Thus, temperature limits larval survival directly through low, lethal temperatures and indirectly through starvation during long periods of sub-lethal temperatures.

The Venosta valley (Province Bozen/Bolzano) stretches in east-west direction; *T. pityocampa* has been occurring at outbreak levels in the secondary *Pinus nigra* stands on the south-facing slope (from 750 to 1250 m elevation) over the last years. The mixed *P. sylvestris* stands on the north-facing slope sustained only very low population densities. Comparison with records of previous surveys carried out by the local forest service showed that the upper limit of *T. pityocampa* has risen from 1150 m in 1975 to 1380 m elevation in 2004.

We recorded climate data during the winter season 2002/03 and 2003/04. Air and larval nest temperature as well as insolation were measured on both, north and south slope at different altitudes. A topoclimatic model was developed for the study area illustrating big differences in temperature on north and south exposed sites, particularly with regard to high temperatures that were favourable for larval feeding during winter. From experiments under laboratory conditions, we estimated threshold temperatures for the nocturnal larval feeding activity. No feeding occurred when night temperatures were kept at -3 °C; larvae fed at night temperatures of 3 °C when they had been activated during photophase by temperatures of 9 °C or 12 °C. Larval nests contributed to a significant increase of daytime temperatures under sunny conditions; depending on nest size and number of larvae inhabiting the nest, temperatures were up to 5 °C higher than air temperatures. Nests had, however, no positive effect on temperature during dark hours. The freezing temperatures of larvae (according to super cooling point measurements) and their starving ability was evaluated under laboratory conditions. Larvae showed no particular adaptation to winter temperatures (freezing occurred at -8 to -11 °C) but 70-80% were able to survive at least 6 weeks without feeding at -5 °C or 0 °C. When kept at night temperatures of -10 °C survival was reduced to 10-30%.

Based on climate data recorded in the field, we calculated the number of hours of potential feeding induction at our study sites in Venosta assuming the threshold of night temperature above 0 °C plus day temperature above 9 °C as revealed in the laboratory experiments. In the period from December 3, 2002, to March 4, 2003, 97 h of potentially induced feeding occurred at the lower study site (elevation 750 m) and 106 h at the upper site (1100 m) on the north-facing slope. Markedly more hours of potentially induced feeding were recorded on the south-facing slope: 476 h at the lower (900 m) and still 265 h at the upper site (1450 m). Based on the topoclimatic model, we extrapolated the potential feeding induction for the whole Venosta study area to highlight areas of favourable climate for the overwintering *T. pityocampa* larvae.

TIPULA PALUDOSA MEIGEN AND *T. OLERACEA* MEIGEN, EUROPEAN CRANE FLIES NEW TO THE EASTERN UNITED STATES: POTENTIALLY SERIOUS TURFGRASS AND PASTURE PESTS

E. Richard Hoebeke and Carolyn Klass

Department of Entomology, Cornell University, Ithaca, NY 14853

Abstract

In early June 2004, grounds personnel of the Niagara County Golf Club in Lockport, NY noticed large numbers of crane flies emerging from the turf. Some flies were collected and sent to the Cornell University Insect Diagnostic Laboratory for identification. They represented one of the European crane flies, *Tipula oleracea* Meigen, which was previously recorded from the Pacific Northwest. This is the first record of this Old World crane fly in eastern North America. In August 2004, the course superintendent of the Niagara Country Club, in Lewiston, NY, also collected crane flies for identification because large numbers were observed emerging from the rough areas of the turf. Interestingly enough, these crane flies were identified as yet another European species, *Tipula paludosa* Meigen, a species previously reported from the Canadian Maritimes, the Pacific Northwest, and the Niagara peninsula of Ontario, Canada. This is the first record of this exotic crane fly from the eastern United States.

Tipula paludosa, a widespread northern European species, was accidentally introduced into Newfoundland and reached the mainland of Canada in northern Nova Scotia (Cape Breton Island) as early as 1955. It was rediscovered again in 1965 in British Columbia and in the Niagara peninsula of Ontario in 1997. *Tipula oleracea*, another common species native to Europe, was first reported from the New World, specifically from Andean Ecuador in 1999, and between 1998 and 1999 it was found in a few locations in western British Columbia, western Washington, and western Oregon.

These two European crane fly species are almost identical in appearance—both are large in stature (1 1/4 to 1 1/2 inches; females generally larger), with grayish brown bodies, and wings slightly cloudy. To distinguish the two from each other, an eye separation character, a wing length character, and genitalic characters can be used. In *T. paludosa*, the eye separation is quite broad, usually several times the width of the basal antennal segment. In sharp contrast, in *T. oleracea* the area between the eyes is very narrow, only as wide as the width of the basal antennal segment. Wings of female *T. paludosa* are shorter than the abdomen. Wings of female *T. oleracea* are clearly longer than the abdomen. Phallic characters are different between the two.

Tipula paludosa and *T. oleracea* are extremely similar biologically. *Tipula paludosa* completes a single generation annually, with adult emergence beginning in late August, and their numbers peaking in September and continuing into October. *Tipula oleracea*, on the other hand, completes two generations annually, with adult emergence in the spring (late May to July) and again in the fall (mid August to late September: for 2004 in NY).

European crane flies are largely turf and pasture pests. *Tipula paludosa* is probably the most injurious and widespread crane fly in northern Europe. In the Pacific Northwest and in Nova Scotia, *T. paludosa* has been found feeding on turf grasses and such hosts as annual and perennial flowers and several types of vegetables and small fruits. In portions of the Niagara peninsula of Ontario, large populations have caused destruction of many home lawns. In a few locations in western British Columbia, and in western Washington and Oregon, *T. oleracea* has become the most serious economic pest of lawns, pastures, and hayfields.

Delimiting surveys for the two species will be conducted in western New York in 2005.

EFFICACY OF MICROWAVE IRRADIATION OF WOOD PALLET MATERIALS FOR ERADICATION OF PINEWOOD NEMATODE AND WOOD-BORING INSECTS

Kelli Hoover[1], Mary Fleming[1,2], Dean Morewood[1,2], Jeff Kimmel[2] and John Janowiak[2]

[1]Department of Entomology, 501 ASI Building, Penn State University, University Park, PA 16802
[2]Department of Forest Resources, 301 Forest Resources Lab, Penn State University University Park, PA 16802

Abstract

Commercialization of microwave systems to eradicate exotics pests infesting wood materials is being considered as a phytosanitary treatment alternative to conventional heating or methyl bromide fumigation to prevent introductions of exotic pests infesting wooden packing materials. Currently, heat treatment and fumigation are the only two phytosanitary treatments internationally approved for solid wood packing materials under the auspices of the United Nations (U.N.). However, the U.N. phytosanitary commission will consider alternative technologies, such as microwave energy, when "sufficient data are available." The goals of this study were to determine the feasibility of killing pinewood nematodes and cerambycids (using cottonwood borers as the test organism) in commercial microwave equipment using temperature as the critical treatment parameter. We also examined the efficacy of microwaves for killing these organisms using a batch processing system versus continuous movement of the target in the field (pass-through microwave or turntable). Our studies using large scale microwave equipment showed that temperatures greater than 62 °C were lethal to both pinewood nematodes (*Bursaphelenchus xylophilus*) and cottonwood borer (CWB) larvae (*Plectrodera scalator*) within red pine lumber under stationary microwave irradiation. Movement through a microwave field increased efficacy of eradication such that all pinewood nematodes and cottonwood borer larvae were killed even when temperatures did not reach 62 °C.

COMPETITIVE ABILITY OF *AILANTHUS ALTISSIMA* AND AN OVERVIEW OF OTHER RWU-4557 INVASIVE PLANT STUDIES

Cynthia D. Huebner

USDA Forest Service, NE Research Station, 180 Canfield St., Morgantown, WV 26505-3101

Abstract

The theme of this year's invasive plant session is invasive plant research conducted by Northeastern Research Station scientists and their collaborators. This theme originated in part from the formation of the Northeastern Research Station Invasive Plant Species Research Network, which currently has 14 members. The mission of this network is to provide a forum where NE research scientists can exchange information, collaborate, and progress more efficiently in their invasive plant research efforts.

My research goals within the RWU-4557 are divided among three broad areas; 1) the genetics, organismal, and population biology of known forest exotic invaders, with an initial focus on *Ailanthus altissima* and *Microstegium vimineum*; 2) defining community vulnerability to invasion; and 3) determining impacts of forest plant invasions on forest communities and ecosystem processes. I am currently working on several questions associated with these goals including:

1) Why are so many exotic invasive plants dioecious?

2) What environmental conditions stimulate root suckering in *A. altissima*

3) Does *A. altissima* have mycorrhizae

4) What environmental conditions are required for germination of *A. altissima* and *M. vimineum*

5) How are *M. vimineum* seed dispersed into forests and what is the rate of spread?

6) What sampling methods best detect early invaders?

7) What environmental and disturbance factors define forest community invasibility?

8) Which forest strata are most susceptible to invasion?

9) How well does *A. altissima* compete with native species under different environmental conditions?

10) Are successful invasions dependent on a seed bank?

11) How are the understories of Eastern hemlock forests responding to hemlock woolly adelgid outbreaks in terms of invasions by exotic plants?

I will now focus on the competitive ability of *A. altissima* question, but first should state that this research is very much a simplified, reductionist approach to a complex problem. The purpose of this research is to evaluate the competitive ability of *A. altissima* in a simulated closed-canopy environment and an open environment against an early-successional species, *Rhus typhina*. *Ailanthus altissima* invades both open areas as well as closed canopy forests, though it appears to have a higher growth rate in open areas, suggesting that high light is optimal for this species. *Rhus typhina* also prefers open areas and like *A. altissima* is dioecious and can spread vegetatively via root suckering. Both intra- and interspecific competition were studied in a controlled greenhouse setting. *Ailanthus altissima* and *Rhus typhina* were grown under a de Wit replacement series experimental design using ample water and nutrients at a total density of 100 seeds per plot in both high light and low light treatments. Allelopathic effects were controlled using activated carbon and none were found. While *R. typhina* had significantly fewer germinants in both high and low light treatments, its root to shoot ratio per individual and average height were significantly greater than that of *A. altissima* in high light. *Ailanthus altissima* appeared to benefit from its negative density effects in low light with regards to competition with *R. typhina*; the fewer germinants appeared to compete better, but did not outperform *R. typhina*. The relative yield results indicate that *R. typhina* is a better competitor than *A. altissima* under high light conditions, but could coexist with *A. altissima* in shaded environments. These results also suggest that *A. altissima* is not inherently better at capturing resources than *R. typhina*, which may provide support for the enemy release hypothesis. Similar experiments are being conducted with the shade-tolerant *Acer rubrum* showing a pattern where the native species is the better competitor in its optimal environment. Future tests varying stressful environmental conditions, mimicking herbivory and pathogens, and ultimately conducting these same tests under field situations are planned.

PRELIMINARY ASSESSMENT OF THE COLD TOLERANCE OF *LARICOBIUS NIGRINUS*, A WINTER-ACTIVE PREDATOR OF THE HEMLOCK WOOLLY ADELGID FROM WESTERN CANADA

Leland M. Humble and Linda Mavin

Natural Resources Canada, Canadian Forest Service, 506 West Burnside Road, Victoria, B.C. Canada V8Z 1M5

Abstract

Laricobius nigrinus Fender is a winter active predator of the hemlock woolly adelgid (HWA), *Adelges tusgae* Annand, native to the Pacific northwest of North America. Adults appear in the foliage of infested hemlocks as the overwintering HWA sistens generation develops (Oct. - Dec.) and begin oviposition in the ovisacs of HWA soon after adelgid oviposition begins in January. Thus, multiple life stages of the predator are present during the coldest periods of the Pacific Northwest winter. As *L. nigrinus* is being evaluated as a biological control agent against HWA in the eastern U.S., where winter climates can be more severe than those of its native range, it is important to understand the cold tolerance of the life stages of the predator present during the winter months.

We assessed the cold tolerance of adults, eggs and larvae of *L. nigrinus* through evaluations of the supercooling points (SCPs) of field-collected adults and laboratory reared (at 5 °C) eggs and larvae. Freezing was fatal to all life stages. The mean SCPs of adults ranged between -16 °C and -19 °C, while those of overwintering one day and five day old eggs were -27.5 °C and -26.9 °C,

respectively. Newly eclosed first instar larvae (L1) that had not yet begun to feed, supercooled to -24 °C, while their supercooling capacity both diminished slightly ($0 = -22.1$ °C) once feeding was intitated. Supercooling capacity diminished with each successive instar, with the SCPs of the L_2, L_3 and L_4 being -17 °C, -15 °C and -13 °C respectively.

Survival of eggs and adults after exposure to sub-zero temperatures above their mean SCPs (-10 °C and -20 °C for eggs; -10 °C and -15 °C for adults) for increasing durations (to a maximum of 8 h) was also evaluated. Survivorship was highest for eggs and adults exposed to -10 °C. Survival of eggs declined with decreasing temperature and increasing duration of exposure. Survival of eggs exposed to -20 °C for 1h was 45%, with no survival evident at longer durations. Increasing durations of exposure of adults to -15 °C (1 ° -4 °C above mean adult SCPs) resulted in reduced adult survival. However, 40% of the adults tested survived 8h exposure to -15 °C. These results indicate that both the duration and extent of extreme winter minima may be determinants of the range of *L. nigrinus* in eastern North America.

EFFECTS OF TIMING OF LARVAL CHILL ON *ANOPLOPHORA GLABRIPENNIS* (COLEOPTERA: CERAMBYCIDAE) SURVIVAL AND PUPATION

Melody A. Keena

USDA Forest Service, Northeastern Research Station, Northeastern Center for Forest Health Research, Hamden, CT 06514

Abstract

Anoplophora glabripennis (Motschulsky) (Coleoptera: Cerambycidae), Asian longhorned beetle, is a recently introduced non-native invasive species in the United States that has the potential to destroy several tree species in urban and forest habitats. The ability to rear *A. glabripennis* in quarantine is critical to rapid progress on techniques for the exclusion, detection, and eradication of this serious pest. Survival and development were compared for larvae from three populations (Ravenswood, Chicago, IL; Bayside, Queens, NY; and Hohhot, Inner Mongolia, China) under four larval treatments (6, 9, 12, or 16 wk at 25 °C followed by 12 wk at 10 °C then returned to 25 °C). Timing of pupation when removed from chill, survival, and successful completion of development were measured for each treatment.

Larvae from the China and Illinois populations were heavier than those from New York. Larvae from the Illinois population began pupation sooner after being removed from the various chill treatments than those from New York or China. Larvae from Illinois also were least affected by the timing of the larval chill period. Pupation success for the China population was highest for individuals with the greatest development time before chill. This result may indicate that larvae from the China population tend to pupate at a later instar, more may require chill to complete development, or some may require more than 1 year to complete development under some conditions. Some larvae from each population did not require a larval chill period to complete pupation. Some larvae from each population that had not reached their critical weight for pupation before the chill period required a second chill period before they initiated pupation. The critical weight for pupation appears to vary both within and between populations, which could indicate a high degree of plasticity or genetic variation for this trait. Overall survival decreased when the developmental time decreased before the chill period. Manipulating the development time before chill appeared to be useful for synchronizing adult emergence and increasing pupation. Further evaluation of the effects of temperature on development is needed to better understand the triggers for pupation and to predict the timing of various life stages for optimal timing of eradication and control treatments. These results indicate that the number of years to complete a generation could be affected by the climate in the location where the beetle is introduced.

ALARM AND OTHER RECENT INITIATIVES ON BIOLOGICAL INVASIONS IN EUROPE

Marc Kenis

CABI Bioscience Switzerland Centre, 2800 Delémont, Switzerland

Abstract

Europe has long been far behind other continents regarding research on biological invasions, probably because Europe has suffered less from plant, animal or pathogen invaders than other regions. However, in the last few years, initiatives on biological invasions have flourished. One of the reasons is the large number of new invasive alien species (IAS) that have established and spread on the continent. In recent years, European have been alerted by the establishment and spread of a high number of IAS, many of which are serious pests elsewhere in the world. New aliens in Europe that have attracted much attention among the public include the western corn rootworm (*Diabrotica virgifera virgifera*), the Asian tiger mosquito (*Aedes albopictus*), the Asian and citrus longhorn beetles (*Anoplophora* spp.), the horse-chestnut leaf miner (*Cameraria ohridella*), the pine wood nematode (*Bursaphelenchus xylophilus*), the American gray squirrel (*Sciurus carolinensis*), several *Phytophthora* spp., fire blight (*Erwinia amylovora*), ragweed (*Ambrosia artemisiifolia*), Japanese knotweed (*Fallopia japonica*), giant hogweed (*Heracleum mantegazzianum*), etc. Consequently, most European countries are now developing national action plans against IAS. At the continental scale, the Council of Europe has just released a "European Strategy against Invasive Alien Species". Regional networks on IAS have been established and more than 10 international conferences on IAS have been organized in Europe in the last 2 years. European research

programs on IAS, mostly funded by the European Union, have been developed. The first projects targeted single IAS, such as the western corn rootworm, the horse-chestnut leaf miner, the pine wood nematode or the giant hogweed. Other projects are now considering the problem of IAS as a whole. One of these projects is ALARM (Assessing Large Scale Environmental Risks for Biodiversity with Tested Methods, 2004-2009), funded by the EU. The main objective of ALARM is to develop an integrated large scale risk assessment to terrestrial and freshwater biodiversity, including risks consequent on climate change, environmental chemicals, biological invasions and rates and extend of loss of pollinators. Within ALARM, 12 European teams work specifically in the biological invasion module. The aims of this module are to (1) assess concurrently both the risks (e.g. likelihood of introduction, establishment and naturalization) and the impacts (ecological and economic consequences) of invasive species; (2) incorporate environmental, historical, cultural and biogeographical data into assessments of the risks and impacts of invasions; (3) introduce a hierarchical perspective of ecosystem vulnerability by examining invasions at local and regional scales; (4) undertake a multidisciplinary approach that involves stakeholders, ecologists, statisticians, modelers and economists, to the problem of ecosystem vulnerability to invasion. Most taxa will be covered, with the notable exception of pathogens.

EFFECTS OF HURRICANE ISABEL ON EASTERN FORESTS: PRELIMINARY FINDINGS

Kerrie L. Kyde[1], Douglas H. Boucher[2*], John L. Snitzer[2], Joyce N. Bailey[3], Christine L. Rodick[2] and Bill Prudden[2]

[1]Maryland Department of Natural Resources, Annapolis, MD 21401
[2]Department of Biology, Hood College, Frederick, MD 21701
[3]Global Ecology Studies Program, Poolesville High School, Poolesville, MD 20837
*E-mail: dboucher@hood.edu

Abstract

Hurricane Isabel made landfall in North Carolina on September 18, 2003, as a Category 2 storm. By the time the storm reached our primary research plot 410 km away in the Maryland Piedmont, Isabel had been downgraded to a tropical storm. At the study site, where a hectare had been established in 1998 in 80- to 100-year-old secondary forest to examine forest growth and regeneration, there were sustained winds of 37 mph and gusts up to 50 mph. Only 5 cm of precipitation was associated with the storm. Despite the relatively weak character of the storm, Isabel did a great deal of damage in the previously established hectare (West Woods - permanent plot), and on six other sites in the Piedmont and the Blue Ridge in Maryland, West Virginia and Virginia.

Following Isabel's passage, we established a 0.4 hectare plot adjacent to the permanent plot, comparable to it in soil type, slope, aspect, forest age and tree species composition. This plot (Less Damaged Plot) sustained much less damage than did the permanent plot. In both plots, we identified downed trees to species, measured tree diameters and heights, and measured the volume and biomass of downed woody debris by the line transect method (Van Wagner 1968, Harmon et al. 1986). In the other six damage sites, we identified to species and measured diameters of downed trees in paired 20 x 100 m damaged and adjacent control transects. In both the permanent and the less damaged plots, we conducted an exotic invasive plant survey in fall 2003 after the storm, identifying 12 species of herbaceous and woody invasive plants, and estimating their percentage cover in 5 x 5m quadrats. Because these species had flowered and fruited earlier in the year, Isabel had not affected their distribution and density; we therefore used this census as an estimate of the invasives present prior to the storm.

We conducted the same census in 2004, scheduled so that quadrats were censused during the same week as in the preceding year. We took simultaneous light readings (photosynthetically active radiation in μg/m2/sec with a LICOR 250) at the southwest corner of each 10 x 10 m quadrat in the Permanent and Less Damaged Plots and in an adjacent field, to measure percentage of full sunlight in the plots. We mapped areas of higher and lower light levels in the permanent plot (gaps and non-gaps). We identified and counted woody seedlings in a subset of quadrats in the permanent plot.

At the West Woods site, 71 of 425 trees greater than 10 cm DBH were uprooted; 21.5% of the total basal area of 36.3 m^2/ha was damaged; treefall was overwhelmingly to the west (225-315°); and canopy height was reduced to less than 5 m at 21.5% of the 10 x 10 m gridpoints in the hectare, whereas previously it had been that low at 1.7% of those points. Trees with larger DBH were more likely to be uprooted. Logistic regression of the binary variable "Uprooted vs. Not Uprooted" showed highly significant effects of DBH (B = 0.042, P < .001). *Prunus serotina* Erhr., black cherry, was uprooted much more frequently than would be expected. Black cherries comprised 15% of the trees in the permanent plot, but accounted for almost 33% of the downed trees. After correcting for DBH, cherry was the only species that showed a significantly higher than expected probability of uprooting (P < .004). Isabel produced literally tons of coarse woody debris in the permanent plot (78.1 Mg/ha), four times the amount present before the hurricane.

We found the same pattern of larger trees blown down at the other six sites. Mean DBH of uprooted trees in 0.2 ha transects was consistently larger than undamaged trees in adjacent control plots (t = 5.89, P (two-tailed) = .002).

Of the 12 exotic invasive species found in the West Woods site in Fall 2003, the most frequent were *Lonicera japonica* Thunb. (88% of quadrats), *Alliaria petiolata* (M. Bieb.) Cavara and Grande (80% of quadrats) and *Rosa multiflora* Thunb. (56% of quadrats). These species were widely distributed, but not especially dense. In most cases, they covered less than 5% of each quadrat. In the 2004 census, we found two species that had been present close to, but not in the plot previously: *Polygonum perfoliatum* L., mile-a-minute, and *Microstegium vimineum* (Trin.) Camus, Japanese stiltgrass. We also found *Polygonum caespitosum* Blume, long-bristled smartweed, an exotic invasive that had not been present anywhere near the plot in 2003.

We compared the change in percentage cover of all invasive plants from 2003 to 2004 in a subset of 45 quadrats from the less damaged plot, and the lower and higher light areas of the permanent plot. The mean change in percentage cover was significantly higher in the high-light areas of the permanent plot than in the low-light areas or the Less Damaged Plot (47.8%, 4.8%, and 4.2%, respectively, Kruskal-Wallis, P <.001). We expect to see the same pattern when the data from all quadrats are analyzed. Most of this difference can be attributed to the change in percentage cover of four species, mile-a-minute, Japanese honeysuckle, long-bristled smartweed and garlic mustard. The percentage cover of the first three increased significantly (Kruskal-Wallis, P < .001, .005 and .002, respectively), and of the last, decreased significantly (P< .001). It is unclear whether the reduction in garlic mustard occurred from shading competition or simply reflects the second year cohort of this biennial species.

The seedlings most frequently found in the permanent plot were:

- *Acer negundo* L., Boxelder (1785/ha),
- *Fraxinus americana* L., White ash (1169/ha)
- *Carya cordiformis* (Wang.) K. Koch, Bitternut hickory (1097/ha)
- *Toxicodendron radicans* (L.) Ktze. (738/ha)
- *Prunus serotina* Erhr., Black cherry (338/ha)

Although *Liriodendron tulipifera* L., yellow-poplar, is the most common adult tree in the plot, (32.5% of 425 stems), we found very few yellow-poplar seedlings. With more light available in the forest, seedlings of this shade-intolerant species may increase in the future.

Work in 2005 will include a spring recensus of native and exotic herbs, a recensus of woody invasives, a fall recensus of exotic invasive plants, measurement of the modification of tree pits and mounds over time and correlation of soil disturbance with invasion, and a complete species census of 36 deer exclosures established in November 2004 in canopy gaps, intact canopy and in an adjacent abandoned agricultural field. The deer exclosure data should help illuminate the impact of browse on post-hurricane succession of natives, invasives and woody seedlings. We expect to expand these censuses to our five additional sites in Maryland.

We predict that as eastern hardwood forests mature and trees increase in size, they are going to become increasingly susceptible to even low-level storm damage, and that the resulting canopy gaps are going to be patchy and larger, rather than limited primarily to single-tree gaps. Further, we expect that forests will become increasingly vulnerable to invasion by exotic species able to take advantage of large disturbances to establish themselves. Yellow-poplar and similar intolerant tree species, which require large gaps for successful recruitment, will become more dominant. Large amounts of coarse woody debris produced by even mild storms may create variations in carbon sequestration rates, as carbon is released from storm-damaged forests and taken up in increased regeneration.

References

Harmon, M.E., J.F. Franklin, F.J. Swanson, P. Sollins, S.V. Gregory, J.D. Lattin, N.H. Anderson, S.P. Cline, N.G. Aumen, J.R. Sedell, G.W. Lienkaemper, K. Cromeck, Jr., and K.W. Cummins. 1986. **Ecology of coarse wood debris in temperate ecosystems.** Advances in Ecological Research Vol 15: 133-302.

Van Wagner, C.E. 1968. **The line intersect method in forest fuel sampling.** Forest Science 14: 20-26.

ALTERNATE METHODS FOR MANAGING ALB POPULATIONS

D.R. Lance[1], J. Francese[1], B. Wang[1], Z. Xu[2], R. Mack[1], V. Mastro[1], and Y. Luo[2]

[1]USDA-APHIS-PPQ-PSDEL, Bldg. 1398, Otis ANGB, MA 02542

[2]College of Natural Resources and Environmental Sciences, Beijing Forestry University, Beijing, PRC

Abstract

Breeding populations of Asian longhorned beetles (ALB), *Anoplophora glabripennis* (Motschulsky), were first discovered in the U.S. in 1996 in Brooklyn, NY. Initially, survey consisted of ground-based visual examination of trees for beetles and their damage, and the only proven control method was the total destruction of infested trees. As part of an overall research effort on the insect, studies on behavior and ecology of adult beetles were initiated in hopes of finding traits that could be exploited to develop improved management methods such as attractant-baited traps, tactics that targeted insecticide applications to the pest (e.g., "attract-and-kill"), trap-tree systems, biologically-based control agents, or improved strategies for employing available methods. Here, we review a group of studies on localized and host-selections behaviors of ALB adults, focusing primarily on work done by USDA-APHIS personnel from the CPHST facility at Otis ANGB, MA. Because ALB populations in the U.S. are typically very sparse and under active eradication, most field work described here was conducted in Ningxia, PRC, in cooperation with researchers at Beijing Forestry University (BFU). Studies that have been conducted in several related areas (e.g., host plant range, longer-range dispersal, sonic detection of insects, evaluation of fungal pathogens) are beyond the scope of this presentation.

In 1999 and 2001, B. Wang and D. Lance ran observational studies to describe patterns of daily activity and localized movement of adult ALB. The 1999, we primarily conducted repeated observations on marked, field-collected beetles that were released into a shelterbelt of poplar hybrids. In 2001, ALB were observed *in situ*, 4 X daily for 3 weeks, in a shelterbelt of poplar and willow. During these studies, we observed quantifiable (significant) trends in daily activity patterns, but we found at least some beetles engaged in all activities and on all portions of trees at all times of day. One exception was the tendency of beetles to remain in shaded areas during hot, sunny periods. Repeated observations of marked beetles on the same tree were common, suggesting limited appetitive movement by these insects. At the same time, though, 10% to 36% of beetles, depending on time and sex, were walking when observed. Observations of flight were rare (unless unduly disturbed, no beetles flew or took flight while being observed), although beetles in general appeared to take flight fairly readily when deprived of requisites such as food, moisture, or shade. Typically, over 50% of beetles were observed on stems larger than those upon which they would normally feed (i.e., > ~7 mm diameter).

Mechanisms of host location and host-plant selection were the subject of several types of studies. In 2000, B. Wang and D. Lance initiated a series of flight-orientation tests in which beetles were released at the center of 7.5-m-diameter ring of eight potted poplar trees. Beetles that left the release point landed on the trees much more often that would have been predicted by chance (based on the proportion of the circle subtended by the trees) and tended to approach the downwind sides of trees (i.e., flying upwind). In addition, when alternating trees were replaced with artificial trees, ALB oriented much more readily to the real trees than to the artificial ones. All of this suggested possible involvement of volatile semiochemicals in orientation of beetles to trees, but results of subsequent trials with cloth-covered real and artificial trees indicated that this orientation was based primarily on visual cues. B. Wang has followed this work with more extensive evaluations of how size, shape, and color affect orientation of ALB to objects. In addition, J. Francese, using a similar technique, was not able to demonstrate that ALB orient preferentially to highly preferred hosts (e.g., *Acer platanoides* of *A. mono*) over more marginal but suitable hosts (e.g., *Populus nigra*) or even comparably-sized artificial trees.

Since 2001, J. Francese has headed a series of complementary studies to determine the possible role of tenure on host plants as a determinant of ALB host utilization patterns. Field-collected beetles were released onto potted hosts of different species, or onto potted artificial trees, and numbers of beetles remaining were counted and specified intervals thereafter. Perhaps surprisingly, there was relatively little difference in beetles remaining on trees over time among *Populus nigra* (considered a good host in Ningxia), *P. alba* (marginal host), and an artificial tree, with low numbers (~10-25%) remaining on trees as little as 8 h after release. Significantly greater proportions of beetles (~50% on average) remained on *Acer* throughout the 8-h period, regardless of whether the trees were hosts that the insect utilizes in N. America or *A. mono*, a species native to Asia. Host selection in this insect appears to occur in large part by visual orientation to a tree followed by the decision to either remain on that tree or move to another.

The role of semiochemicals in the ecology of ALB remains, for the most part, poorly defined, despite ongoing research in this area since the insect's discovery in the U.S. This work has been conducted primarily by scientists at SUNY-ESF in Syracuse, NY, USDA-ARS in Beltsville, MD (and more recently Newark, DE), Beijing Forestry University, and, more peripherally, the APHIS lab at Otis. GC-EAD studies have been run by several of these groups and resulted in the identification of numerous antennally active compounds both from the beetles and from their host plants. Unfortunately, results of laboratory and field bioassays of these materials have yet to demonstrate the existence of a volatile attractant that is sufficiently effective for program use, but components of a contact pheromone for mate recognition have been identified (see Zhang et al., *Naturwissenschaften* 90: 410 [2003]) and more recently tested host-plant blends continue to show some promise in tests being run by USDA-ARS scientists.

Although we still lack an effective method to attract beetles to traps, tests since 2002 have worked toward developing a trap that exploits the beetles' relatively frequent walking on larger stems. Commercially available traps such as the IPM Tech Intercept Panel trap (used as a standard) and Great Lakes IPM plum curculio trap (modified for the larger ALB) have been tested, along several experimental traps designed by Otis or BFU personnel. Of traps tested to date, the Great Lakes IPM trap appears most useful, as it is commercially available, relatively simple to use, and at least comparable to others in trapping power (captures several-fold more than the IPM Tech trap, for example). In 2004 mark-recapture studies, though, we found that the Great Lakes IPM trap captured only ~10% of beetles that were placed on the same tree as the trap, and that the proportion dropped to ~2% for trees as little as 4 m from the trap. Of the 600 beetles in this study, two were captured on trees that were 100 to 150 m from their release sites.

We also attempted to exploit beetle movement on trunks of trees for control by applying insecticides to limited portions of trees (specifically, bands around larger stems). We initially chose test compounds based on results of previous insecticide trials of B. Wang and co-workers. In some cases, burlap was soaked in label-rate aqueous mixtures of commercially available formulations (e.g., "Tempo"; a.i. = cyfluthrin), allowed to air-dry, and stapled (30-cm bands) around trees. In other cases, cooperators provided experimental formulations (e.g., IPM Tech, Hercon Environmental, Isca Tech). In general, effective a.i.'s (cyfluthrin, lambda-cyhalothrin, and, to a lesser extent, permethrin), produced significantly greater numbers of dead beetles around treated versus untreated trees. Unfortunately, we have not been able to show that this translates into significantly fewer live beetles on the trees, even in 2004 testing where larger plots (e.g., 20 trees long in a shelter belt) were used in an attempt to reduce effects of beetle movement on populations in individual trees. Bioassays (2004) of treated burlap (using the surrogate species *Plectrodera scalator*) indicated that the required exposure time for cyfluthrin (the compound we have evaluated most intensively in these tests) may be longer than desirable for effective control. Exposure to cyfluthrin-treated burlap for 5 min produced mortality that was roughly comparable to a 1-min exposure to lambda-cyhalothrin, so a switching to this "hotter" insecticide may prove helpful (tests need to be repeated with *A. glabripennis*).

Finally, R. Mack and co-workers demonstrated trapping and insecticide-banding methods in Brooklyn, NY and Carteret, NJ in 2004. No beetles were recorded as trapped or killed at the two Brooklyn sites, but this was not unexpected as one of the sites (Evergreens Cemetery) had no known infestation, and materials at the other (a courtyard behind row-houses on Grand Avenue) were in place for only a week, relatively late in the season, before the trees were removed. By contrast, in Carteret, NJ, nine dead beetles were found in conjunction with insecticide-banded trees (either Demand [lambda-cyhalothrin] on burlap or cypermethrin in "Splat", an Isca Tech product; 5 trees treated with each). One of the nine was found in a hanging device designed to trap falling beetles; the others were found on the ground. Also, five beetles were captured in modified Great Lakes IPM traps that were installed above fungus-treated bands on 10 trees. Four of those were send to A. Hayek (Cornell Univ.), but she was unable to confirm the presence of fungal infections in those insects.

In conclusion, attempts to develop alternative management tactics based on behavior of adult ALB have not, to date, produced any "magic bullets" for the eradication programs. However, trapping methods and, especially following optimization, insecticide-banding methods may prove useful for specific management goals.

We wish to thank the USDA-APHIS-PPQ, New York State, and New Jersey Asian Longhorned Beetle Eradication Programs for assistance in performing the U.S.-based portions of the field studies described in here.

CHLORTETRACYCLINE ENHANCES SURVIVAL OF LARVAL ANOPLOPHORA GLABRIPENNIS REARED ON ARTIFICIAL DIET

D.R. Lance and B.S. Holske

USDA-APHIS-PPQ-PSDEL, Bldg. 1398, Otis ANGB, MA 02542

Abstract

During production of Asian longhorned beetles, *Anoplophora glabripennis* (ALB), in the Otis Insect Quarantine Facility, problems with microbial (especially bacterial) contamination of the artificial larval diet were recurrent, despite attempts to introduce aseptic techniques into rearing protocols. This contamination appeared to be causing reduced survival of immature stages to the point where sustainability of the colony was, at times, jeopardized. In 2003, we initiated a study to see if addition of chlortetracycline-HCL could alleviate this problem. In the first generation of the test, addition of chlortetracycline-HCL at either 0.14% or 0.28% by weight of Ogura diet increased the survival of established larvae from 26% (to pupation) and 4% (to adult) on control diet to >60%. Establishment of neonates was low (~40% mortality before the first diet change) in the first generation, regardless of diet treatment. In the second generation, improved handling and related procedures boosted establishment to >90% of larvae for all treatments. By 90 d into the second generation, however, mortality was already significantly greater for the control diet (~30%) than for the diet with antibiotic (still <10%). Adding antibiotic appeared to have little effect on development rate or weight of larvae. Our results to date suggest that addition of an antibiotic such as chlortetracycline to artificial diets for ALB larvae can substantially reduce dietary contamination and produce major improvements in survival. This may appear counter-intuitive, as microbial gut symbionts are typically thought to be important in the nutrition of wood-infesting insects. Additional handling and scheduling changes also produced sizeable improvements in survival and establishment of neonates on artificial diet.

COMMERCIALLY AVAILABLE TRAPS AND LURES FOR DETECTING NUN MOTH, *LYMANTRIA MONACHA* L., IN NORTH AMERICA

D.R. Lance[1], P.W. Schaefer[2], A.J. Sawyer[1], V.C. Mastro[1], J. Gonschorrek[3], M. Kolb[3], L. Sukovata[4] and G. Yurchenko[5]

[1]USDA-APHIS-PPQ-PSDEL, Bldg. 1398, Otis ANGB, MA 02542
[2]USDA-ARS-BIIR, 501 S. Chapel St., Newark, DE 19713
[3]Hessen-Forst, Forsteinrichtung Information, Versuchswesen, Prof.-Oelkers-Straße 6, D-34346 Hann. Münden, Germany
[4]Forest Research Institute, 3, Bitwy Warszawskeij 1920 str., 00-973 Warsaw, Poland
[5]Far East Forestry Research Institute, 71, Volochaevskaya St., Khabarovsk, 680020, Russia

Abstract

Studies were conducted to identify commercially available traps and lures that were suitable for use in detecting incipient populations of nun moth, *Lymantria monacha* L. Volatile components of the various lure formulations included only (+)-disparlure [(7R, 8S)-cis-7,8-epoxy-2-methyloctadecane], only (±)-disparlure, or a 20:20:1 blend of (±)-disparlure, (±)-monachalure [cis-7,8-epoxy-octadecane], and 2-methyl-Z7-octadecene. Tests were run in several locations throughout the range of *L. monacha*, including Japan, Korea, the Russian Far East, Poland, and Germany. In both Europe and Asia, capture of male *L. monacha* in traps with 410 µg of the 20:20:1 blend, formulated in a polyurethane tube (Phero Tech), was comparable to or somewhat greater than capture in traps with 500 µg of (±)-disparlure in a plastic laminate formulation (Hercon); Phero Tech lures that were formulated with 41 µg of the 20:20:1 blend or (in Asia only) Hercon lures with 500 µg of (+)-disparlure attracted significantly fewer *L. monacha*. In addition, traps baited with the 20:20:1 blend caught far fewer gypsy moths, *L. dispar* L., when compared to traps with any of the disparlure-only baits. Standard delta traps appeared suitable for use on *L. monacha*, although slight modifications to standard methods (for gypsy moth survey) of trap folding and hanging improved catch. Relative numbers of male *L. monacha* captured in Europe and Asia by the various commercial lures differed from predictions based on results of earlier studies, suggesting that the chemical ecology of adult *L. monacha* is still not fully understood.

METHOD FOR THE EXTRACTION AND ANALYSIS OF IMIDACLOPRID RESIDUES IN PLANT MATERIAL BY ENZYME-LINKED IMMUNOSORBENT ASSAY (ELISA)

Phillip A. Lewis, John J. Molongoski and Jessica Hagan

USDA-APHIS, Otis Plant Protection Laboratory, Bldg 1398, Otis ANGB, MA 02542-5008

Abstract

Residues of the pesticide imidacloprid in plant tissue are typically determined by extraction of the sample in an organic solvent followed by analysis of the pesticide residue by either HPLC or GC-MS. These methods, while accurate, are expensive and time consuming to perform and are not convenient for the processing of large numbers of samples. An Enzyme Linked Immuno-sorbent Assay (ELISA) is commercially available which can rapidly analyze large numbers of samples with great sensitivity and at reduced cost. Presently, this assay is restricted to the determination of imidacloprid residues in aqueous samples. We have successfully utilized this method to measure imidacloprid concentrations in the xylem sap of pesticide treated trees. In order to expand the capabilities of our residue analysis, we set out to develop techniques whereby the ELISA assay could be utilized to quantify residues from the solvent-extracted phloem or leaves of imidacloprid-treated trees. Our objective is to develop a rapid and reliable method for measuring imidacloprid concentrations in specific plant tissues targeted and fed upon by plant pests such as the Asian longhorned beetle (ALB) or the emerald ash borer (EAB).

The percentage recovery of imidacloprid added to ash phloem tissue ranged from 89 to 119% over a range of 48 to 1600 ng of added pesticide. All of the pesticide residue recovered was found in the initial methanol extraction and subsequent wash. No detectable imidacloprid was found in the second methanol extraction. The LOQ of imidacloprid from the plugs under the extraction conditions we utilized (4 ml initial methanol extraction and 40 X dilution of the sample with distilled water prior to ELISA analysis) was approximately 48 ng. A dilution of tissue extracts less than 40 X yielded positive matrix effects on the assay, resulting in false positive values. The efficiency of recovery of imidacloprid from methanol extracted Norway maple leaves was excellent (93.5 and 94.5% respectively for the two concentrations of imidacloprid tested). Unlike the phloem extracts, however, only 90 to 92% of the added imidacloprid was recovered in the first extraction and subsequent wash step. The remaining 8 to 10 % of the added imidacloprid was recovered in the second methanol extraction. This suggests that a more strenuous extraction technique may be required to quantitatively recover imidacloprid from leaf tissue in a single extraction procedure.

Our results demonstrate that a simple methanol extraction can be coupled with a commercially available ELISA kit to provide a suitable screening method for the quantitative determination of imidacloprid in the phloem or leaf tissue of ash and maple trees. In addition, as employed, the method does not require any extensive sample clean-up leading to a considerable savings in time and cost.

MODELING THE SPREAD OF ASIAN LONGHORNED BEETLE IN NEW YORK CITY

Jacqueline W.T. Lu[1,2] and Gareth J. Russell[1]

[1]Columbia University, Department of Ecology, Evolution and Environmental Biology, 10th Floor Schermerhorn Ext., 1200 Amsterdam Avenue, New York, NY 10027
[2]City of New York, Department of Parks & Recreation, Central Forestry & Horticulture, Olmsted Center, Flushing Meadow Corona Park, Flushing, NY 11368

Abstract

Introduction

The goal of this project was to develop a model that describes the local infestation dynamics of the Asian longhorned beetle *Anoplophora glabripennis* (ALB) in Bayside, New York City, using data on infested trees and uninfested host trees from the New York Eradication Program. In most epidemiological data there is uncertainty about the timing of events, such as the time a host was first infested, first contagious to others, or removed and no longer contagious. In the case of ALB, uncertainty exists because of our inability to precisely 'backdate' the time of first exit from the level of damage observed on the infested tree. The use of a likelihood approach, combined with integration over timing uncertainty, allowed us to build models incorporating several factors that may affect the pattern of ALB spread. Information based statistics allowed us to directly compare and select the model best supported by the observed data. The selected model may then be applied to both management and research applications.

From Program Data to Estimated Infestation Events for Modeling

The New York Asian Longhorned Beetle Eradication Program records the date each infested tree was found, the date the infested tree was removed, and a damage code based on the level of damage observed. We used a previously developed relationship between damage level and the age of an infestation, based on a Jersey City outbreak discovered in October 2002 (Sawyer et al. 2004), to 'backdate' the timings of infestation events in a Bayside, NYC outbreak. For six of the infested Jersey City trees, Sawyer et al. (2004) used the numbers of growth rings around exit holes to calculate the periods of time during which each tree must have been first infested and when it was first potentially able to infest other trees. These trees represented each damage code that was recorded, as well as the four

earliest and most heavily damaged trees (the oldest exit hole found was made in 1998). Because Jersey City trees that were classified into the same damage code were found through dissection to have been infested in different years, the backdating algorithm can at best give an interval within which each tree was likely to have been infested. This means that there is also an interval within which beetles will have first begun to emerge and possibly infest other trees (Figure 1).

Uncertain Timing and the Use of Likelihood Models

In most epidemiological data there is uncertainty about the timing of events, such as when a node is first infested, first contagious, and first removed or no longer contagious (t_n, c_n and r_n). We incorporated such uncertainty into a likelihood model of the spread of an infestation based on a 'distance' matrix D and associated distance function $f(d_{ij})$. The distance function converts an element of D into a transmission rate T_{ij}. Our model considers the problem of fitting various models to data of an epidemic spread of an infection on a set of nodes n = 1, 2, 3, . . . , N with fixed spatial relationships to one

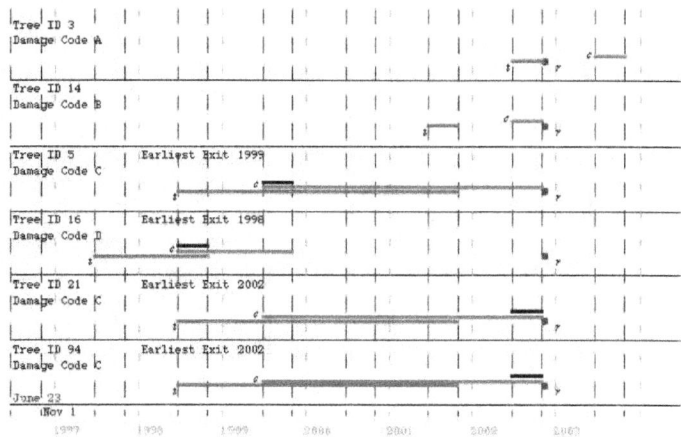

Figure 1.—Calculation of t_n and c_n intervals for Jersey City trees and comparison to earliest date of exit as determined from dissections.

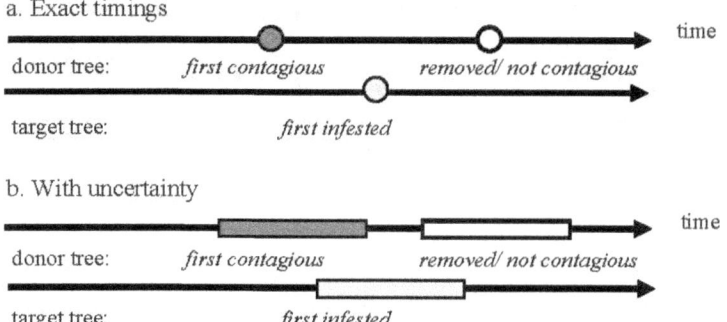

a. Exact timings

time

donor tree: *first contagious* *removed/ not contagious*

target tree: *first infested*

b. With uncertainty

time

donor tree: *first contagious* *removed/ not contagious*

target tree: *first infested*

Figure 2.—Overlaps in infestation events between a donor tree and a target tree.

another; in the case of ALB, these nodes are individual trees. So, this is a spatially explicit model that considers the density of available hosts and their relationships to infested trees. The best-fit parameters for the distance function are those that maximize the likelihood of the observed ALB dataset.

If we knew the timing of infestation events exactly, we would be able to calculate the probability a target tree i was not infested by a donor tree j as $P = e^{T_{ij}(r_j - c_j)}$ (the probability of drawing zero from a Poisson distribution with rate parameter $T_{ij}(r_j - c_j)$ - Figure 2a). We can then calculate the probability of at least one infestation as $1 - P$.

With uncertainty, however, first infestation occurs during an interval, and the contagious period of a donor tree is also an interval with uncertain beginning and end (Figure 2b). Our list of $\{t_n, c_n, r_n\}$ event triples for each node becomes a list of 'pair-triples' $\{\{t_{n,1}, t_{n,2}\}, \{c_{n,1}, c_{n,2}\}, \{r_{n,1}, r_{n,2}\}\}$. To calculate the probabilities we therefore have to integrate over this uncertainty, which we do under the assumption that no time within each interval is more likely than any other. Depending on how the intervals overlap (there are 15 possible combinations in the general model), calculating the probability of infestation can involve a combination of double and single integrals. The product of the probabilities of infestation for each infested tree during the contagious intervals of all the other infested trees, and the probabilities of no infection for uninfested trees, gives the likelihood of the entire dataset (for further details on the general model, see Russell and Lu in prepsaration). The general model was adapted to specifically analyze the Bayside infestation

data from New York City, where there was no uncertainty about the removal date.

Model Fitting to Bayside, New York

We initially fitted four different distance functions to the backdated infestation data in Bayside, New York. Limitations in computing speed and memory prevented the calculation of all the pairwise probabilities for every tree in the data at once, so we created spatially nested subsets of the entire dataset and fit the models to each. A search function was used to calculate the maximum likelihood estimates of the fitted parameters. The MLEs were similar across data set extents for each distance function except the exponential decay ($f(d_{ij}) = ae^{-bd}$), so model selection was limited to the remaining three distance functions.

Maximum likelihood models are a natural approach for dealing with probabilistic infestation data. Furthermore, information-based statistics like Akaike's Information Criterion (AIC) allow comparison of multiple models with different levels of complexity (Burnham and Anderson 2002). Table 1 shows the results of the model selection process for the three distance functions. AIC is defined as $-2 \log L + 2 V$, where L is the maximized likelihood of a candidate model with V free parameters. Comparison of AIC values chose the radius decay distance function (lowest AIC value) as the model that was best supported by the data.

Simulations and Potential Tools

Using data on host tree locations throughout New York City, we created a risk map of ALB spread by performing simulations of spread using the selected distance model.

Table 1.—Maximum likelihood and AIC values for fitted models.

Model name	$f(d_{ij})$	Max. likelihood L	AIC value
Radius	a/d	-85.235	172.47
Radius decay	$a*e^{-bd}/d$	-69.0487	142.097
Radius power	ad^{-b}	-77.1233	158.247

The host tree population was divided into cells, into each of which a single infestation was seeded. We simulated the spread of an infestation until 50 trees in each cell were infested, recording the duration of the simulation (Map 1). The risk map is visually similar to a map of host tree density, which is not surprising given that our model is a simple distance function. Nevertheless, the risk map provides a quantitative measure that could help inform managers of the level of survey that would need to be done before an area could be declared uninfested. This is especially important in a pest with a high detection threshold such as the ALB; in an area where ALB spreads more slowly, a higher level of survey effort would be required.

Neighborhood-scale simulations were also performed on Bayside's host tree data and compared to the observed progression of the infestation. Trees that were infested in the greatest proportion of the simulations were the trees that were also infested earliest in the real data. There was

more variation in the proportion of simulations in which infestation occurred for trees that were infested later, but this is expected because the timing of later events is strongly affected by the stochastic nature of the early stages of spread when just a few trees are infested. These simulations also identified areas that were only infested in the simulations and not actually found infested, and vice versa. Differences between model predictions and observations may be due to the role of other factors in dispersal, such as ALB host preference or the role of buildings as barriers to dispersal. Simulations at this scale may also be used to guide program managers to areas where more survey is required, by locating areas where simulated infestations occurred but where none have been reported to date.

Future Directions and Other Applications

Future work will add other factors that may affect dispersal to the basic distance functions fitted above. Because the distance function converts an element of D (in this case the distance between two trees) into a transmission rate T_{ij}, the matrix D does not have to be an actual distance, but can be an 'effective' distance representing the relative difficulty of transmission between trees due to host preference and environmental characteristics. The general model may also be applied to a variety of types of uncertain epidemiological data. One such type is 'regular census' data, where infestations occur at some unknown time in the interval between surveys (survey uncertainty). Timing uncertainty may also be due to incomplete knowledge of an organism's biology, such as the duration of an incubation period before a node is contagious, or before it is no longer contagious (biological uncertainty). This study is an example of how imperfect operational data can nevertheless contribute to research in factors affecting invasive species spread, and generate results which can be used in turn as management tools for program managers.

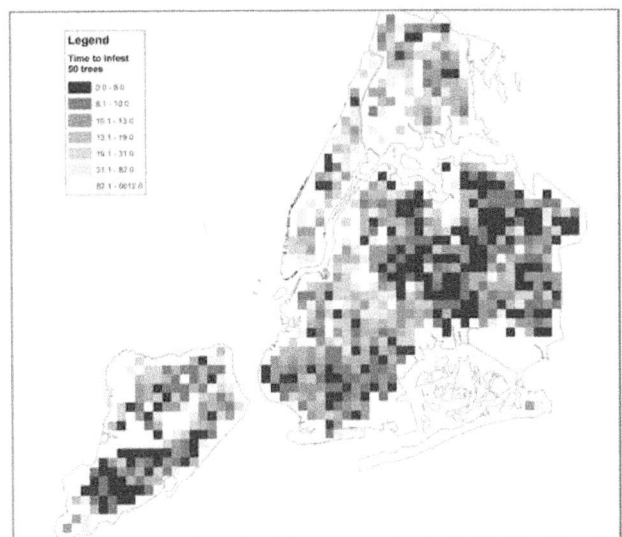

Map 1.—Simulations of selected model on hosts in New York City. Dark areas have faster rates of spread.

References

Burnham, K.P., and D.R. Anderson. 2002. **Model selection and multimodel inference : a practical information-theoretic approach, 2nd edition.** Springer, New York.

Russell, G.J., and J. W.T. Lu. 2004. **Modeling the spread of an epidemic under timing uncertainty.** In prep.

Sawyer, A.J., V.C. Mastro, B.C. Emens, and T. Denholm. 2004. **Analysis of the Asian longhorned beetle infestation in Jersey City, NJ**, poster. 2004 USDA Interagency Research Forum on Gypsy Moth and other Invasive Species, Annapolis MD.

REDUCTION IN REPRODUCTION AND PATHOGEN TRANSMISSION DURING MATING BY ASIAN LONGHORNED BEETLE (*ANOPLOPHORA GLABRIPENNIS*) ADULTS INFECTED WITH *METARHIZIUM ANISOPLIAE*

Jennifer Lund and Ann E. Hajek

Dept. Entomology, Cornell University, Comstock Hall, Ithaca NY

Abstract

The Asian longhorned beetle, Anoplophora glabripennis is an invasive, exotic pest of hardwoods in the U.S. and Canada. The fungal pathogen *Metarhizium anisopliae* has been shown to readily infect adult beetles in laboratory and field (Dubois 2003, Hajek & Lund, unpubl. data). We designed experiments to 1) test the effect of *M. anisopliae* fungal infection on fecundity of female adult beetles; 2) test the effect of fungal infection on the longevity of adult beetles; 3) determine whether adult females transfer this pathogen to males during mating; and 4) determine whether adult females transfer this pathogen to eggs and larva.

Female beetles were exposed to fungal cultures and then caged with a non-inoculated male beetle, *Acer saccharum* twigs and bolt from an *A. saccharum* sapling for one week. Beetles were checked daily for death and examined weekly for infection. Three weeks after the oviposition week, larvae and unhatched eggs were removed from bolts and counted and larvae were placed on artificial diet. One month later, larvae were checked for death and dead larvae were examined for signs of fungal infection.

Control adult female beetles took longer to die then infected females (25.8 days versus 10.6 days). Nearly 94% of adult male beetles died from infections after being placed with an inoculated adult female beetle. Male beetles paired with infected females died significantly sooner than those paired with control females (19.2 days versus 42.5 days). Average fecundity was lower for infected females after inoculation (4.4 eggs/female) than for control beetles (13.0 eggs/female). Fewer eggs hatched from infected females (70.2%) versus healthy females (77.8%). Larvae from infected beetles experienced greater mortality (74.2 %) and had a higher incidence of infection (37.5 %) than control larvae (48.9 % and 0.4 %). Based on egg hatch and larval survival, on average inoculated females produced 0.8 offspring that survived 6 weeks after oviposition while control females produced 5.2.

In conclusion, *M. anisopliae*-inoculated females have shortened longevity and can pass spores to other adults, as well as to the eggs and larvae it produces. We feel that *M. anisopliae* is a well rounded control agent and not only reduces the adult life span, thus reducing the number of eggs laid, but also lowers the viability of offspring the female produces while she is still alive.

THE BIOLOGY AND PHENOLOGY OF THE EMERALD ASH BORER

D. Barry Lyons and Gene C. Jones

Natural Resources Canada, Canadian Forest Service, 1219 Queen Street East, Sault Ste. Marie, Ontario Canada P6A 2E5

Abstract

Emergence of adults of the emerald ash borer (EAB), *Agrilus planipennis* Fairmaire, from caged ash logs, at a marshalling yard in Essex Co., Ontario, began during the first week in June in 2003 and peaked in late June. A few adults were observed flying in the marshalling yard on 28 May. Median emergence dates were 25 June for males and 26 June for females. In 2004, median emergence dates were 11 June and 12 June for males and females, respectively. Sex ratio of emerging adults approached unity for 2003, but was skewed towards males (58.5%) in 2004. The logs from which the beetles emerged had an unknown thermal history and may have been exposed to direct sunlight for considerable periods of time. Thus, these emergence data probably reflect emergence comparable to that expected from exposed urban landscape trees. In three mature woodlots, adults captured on TangleTrap™-coated sticky traps, on host trees at ca. 2 m above the ground, demonstrated considerable woodlot-to-woodlot and year-to-year variation in numbers and activity periods. In one heavily-infested plot, 50 traps captured ca. 7000 beetles during the flight period in both years. With the exception of one lightly infested plot in 2003, traps captured a preponderance of females (66.1- 88.9%). For both years, peak activity periods were inversely correlated with crown density of the woodlots. For the three plots trapped in 2003, interpolated median emergence dates were 3, 10 and 13 July, while median dates for the same three plots in 2004 occurred earlier on 21, 27 June and 4 July.

Tangle-trap-coated traps on green ash (*Fraxinus pennsylvanica* Marsh.), basswood (*Tilia americana* L.), silver maple (*Acer saccharinum* L.) and shagbark hickory (*Carya ovata* (Mill.) K. Koch) captured an average of 161.4, 1.6, 3.3, and 2.7 emerald ash borer adults per 0.25 m2 of surface area. This highly significant difference between captures on host trees and non-host trees strongly suggests that the beetles are responding to some cue provided by the host and are not landing on trees at random to determine their suitability for oviposition.

The size distribution of peristoma (sclerotized region around the mouthparts) widths of larvae of EAB dissected from host logs, were determined using an ocular micrometer, This distribution exhibited four well defined modes, indicating four larval instars. Lower size limits of peristoma widths for instars II, III, and IV were 0.325, 0.550 and 0.975 mm. Peristoma widths of prepupae dissected from logs fell within the size limits of IVth instar larvae, but the majority of these widths was skewed towards the upper size limit of the mode. This trend probably reflects the larger sizes of females and their later emergence during the period that we sampled. Temporal distribution of larval instars based on peristoma measurements showed progressive development. Late in the growing season the majority of the population was in the prepupal stage, but a small proportion of the population was in earlier instars. This suggests that some of the population enters winter in the larval stage. A small proportion of the population was also observed in early spring in the larval stage, suggesting that these individuals survived winter as larvae. These observations have implications for the duration of a generation.

EAB-infested green ash bolts were collected in winter and after a storage period at low temperature, bolts were placed in cages at one of six constant temperatures (18-33 °C) in the laboratory. The cages containing the bolts were examined daily for adult emergence. Linear functions were fitted to the median temperature-dependent emergence rates from the logs, independently for male and female adults. For both males and females the estimated developmental threshold was 13.5 °C, and emergence for males and females required 303.0 and 344.8 DD, respectively, above this threshold. For each rearing temperature, emergence was normalized by dividing emergence times by median emergence time. The normalized times for all temperatures were pooled separately for males and females and a weibull functions were fitted to the normalized times to describe the variability around the median emergence rates. The rate functions and these variability functions were incorporated into a simple phenology model to predict adult emergence. Air temperatures provided by Environment Canada for the Windsor airport for 2003 and 2004 were used as model input. This model adequately predicted the beginning of adult activity in the woodlots for both years, but was unable to predict emergence from the logs in the marshalling yard. Microclimatic temperatures under the bark in these logs exposed to direst solar radiation would be considerably greater than temperatures recorded in a standard weather station. Conversely, temperatures within a closed canopy woodlot would more closely approximate ambient air temperatures.

However, post-winter development of EAB in host trees consists of three distinct processes or phenophases. These are the prepupal period which culminates in pupation, the pupal period that ends at adult eclosion, and a teneral adult period that includes the process of sclerotization and a period of inactivity. Each process may have different developmental rate and threshold parameters, potentially complicating predictions based a models that incorporates all three processes combined, such as the one described above. To examine these individual processes in the laboratory we extracted prepupae from ash trees in winter and after a chilling period, we reared the prepupae at six constant temperatures in the laboratory. Linear functions were fitted to individual rates for the three processes for both males and females. For male and female prepupal periods the developmental thresholds were 12.0 and 11.5 °C and the heat accumulation requirements for development were 118.3 and 121.0 DD above these thresholds, respectively. For pupal periods, the thresholds were 13.6 and 14.7 °C with heat accumulations of 139.2 and 114.6 DD above the thresholds, respectively. Thresholds of 13.6 and 10.1 °C, with DD accumulations

of 43.1 and 64.4 described the development of teneral adults. Whether the latter reflects the true behavior of the beetle in the pupal chambers in/under the bark remains to be determined. The pupal period was less variable than the other phenophases as reflected by higher r^2 values for these regressions. Consequently, development is probably more rigorously defined for the pupal stage. For all three phenophases, development thresholds are relatively high and reasonably consistent, thus the use of combined processes in the phenology model described above is probably justified. A rate function and a variability function have also been constructed for egg development of EAB. This stage also had a high development threshold of 13.9 °C with a degree-day requirement of 155.2 above this threshold for completion of development.

To determine the longevity of adults, males and females were housed separately in plastic-cup rearing cages and provided with access to water and fresh foliage. The cages were then placed in one of seven constant temperature chambers (12 to 33 °C). At most temperatures and under these conditions, male and female longevity was comparable. For temperatures of 18°C or greater, longevity was inversely correlated with temperature. At 12 and 15 °C reductions in feeding rates negatively affected longevity. At 18, 21, 24, 27 and 33 °C, median longevities for females were 102.5, 38.0, 22.5, 19.0, and 5.0 days, respectively.

Mating pairs confined in plastic-cup rearing containers at 24 °C, as described above were observed daily for egg production and mating. There was a highly significant linear relationship between the time to first observed mating and the time to first oviposition. No matings or ovipositions were observed until at least 12 days after adult eclosion, with means for both events of ca. 23 days post eclosion.

THE EFFECTS OF TIMBER HARVESTING AND PRESCRIBED FIRE ON INVASIVE PLANT DYNAMICS IN THE CENTRAL APPALACHIANS

Michael A. Marsh[1], Mary Ann Fajvan[2], Cynthia D. Huebner[2], and Thomas M. Schuler[3]

[1]Division of Forestry, West Virginia University, 322 Percival Hall, Morgantown, WV 26506-6125
[2]USDA Forest Service, Forestry Sciences Laboratory, 180 Canfield St., Morgantown, WV 26505-3101
[3]USDA Forest Service, Timber and Watershed Laboratory and the Fernow Experimental Forest, Rt. 219N, Parsons, WV 26287

Abstract

Land managers throughout the central Appalachian region are using prescribed fire to restore table mountain pine (*Pinus pungens* Lamb.), pitch pine (*Pinus rigida* Mill.), and oak (*Quercus* spp. L.) forest communities. However, there is little knowledge of the relationship between prescribed fire and forest invasion by exotic plants. The objective of our study is to examine the relationships between prescribed fire and the abundance of exotic, invasive plants on three similar mountains representing a chronosequence of time since burning. Our sites are located in the Dry River Ranger District of the George Washington National Forest, WV. The mountains were burned at different times: Brushy Knob (BK) treated in 1992, Heavener Mountain (HM) treated in 2003, and Dunkle Knob (DK) treated in 2004. In addition, timber harvesting occurred at scattered locations on all the mountains during the 1970s and early 1980s. Each mountain was stratified by northeast and southwest aspects and lower and upper elevations for vegetation sampling beginning in 2003. Initial (2003) vegetation inventories of DK (pre-burn), BK and HM (post-burn) as well as personal observations indicate that exotic invasive plants such as Ailanthus (*Ailanthus altissima* (Mill.) Swingle) and garlic mustard (*Alliaria petiolata* (M. Bieb.) Cavara & Grande) were primarily restricted to areas where logging occurred (i.e. coves and lower slopes) and other disturbed areas such as firelines.

Following prescribed fire on DK (2004), mean percent cover of garlic mustard remained unchanged, possibly due to the fire missing a couple of plots where this species was inventoried in 2003. *Ailanthus* seedlings were inventoried in three out of the four sections, but only one (the northeast upper elevation section) showed a significant increase. However, field observations indicate that *Ailanthus* seedlings were not just restricted to burned areas on DK, hence the sampling design did not capture the true abundance of the propagules of this exotic tree. Field observations in 2004 also suggest an increase in number of ailanthus seedlings on HM, but not on BK. The preliminary results of this study support the need for monitoring problematic non-native species in prescribed burning programs. Additional research is also needed to test and improve sampling methods for documenting exotic invasive plant dynamics in response to fire and other disturbances.

ECOSENTINEL™: A DECISION SUPPORT TOOL FOR PEST MONITORING IN SIBERIA AND THE RUSSIAN FAR EAST

Bruce J. Miller[1], Yuri A. Baranchikov[2] and Max W. McFadden[1]

[1]The Heron Group, LLC, PO Box 741, Georgetown, DE 19947
[2]V.N. Sukachev Institute of Forest, Siberian Branch, Russian Academy of Sciences, Academgorodok, Krasnoyarsk 660036, Russia

Abstract

A new decision support software tool, EcoSentinel™ —a proprietary software application—can help decision makers address and respond to complex social, natural resource, and environmental problems including famine onset, human health hotspots, insect pest outbreaks that affect important forest or agricultural resources, and status of threatened and endangered species or whole ecosystems such as forests. EcoSentinel™ can process both satellite imagery and geographically referenced data (e.g., identified with longitude and latitude) into maps designed to predict potential outcomes in the overall problem context (e.g., forest loss, insect outbreaks, forest fire, slash and burn, agricultural extensification).

EcoSentinel™ uses a knowledge base (i.e., a formalized articulation of a model's logic). The knowledge base can process any type of data including geographically referenced data which can be used to create maps showing predicted outcomes of the problem articulated in the model, including input data collected from specific points or places. EcoSentinel™ then processes these data into suitable two-dimensional geographically referenced (map) format. These maps are suitable for use in all geographic information systems (GIS).

One example of an EcoSentinel™ model is EcoSentinel/ SM developed for the USAID/Russia-funded FOREST project. EcoSentinel/SM, The Siberian Moth Outbreak Prediction Model, is a knowledge base that captures the equations and logic of Dr. Yuri Kondakov's career-long research on forest defoliation and outbreak prediction of Siberian moth in the Taiga Forests of Siberia. This model consists of two predictive models: a defoliation prediction model based on Siberian moth larvae observations, and a potential outbreak prediction model based on measured changes in Siberian moth adult populations and factors related to reproduction. The Siberian Moth Outbreak Prediction Model uses Kriging to smooth both moth capture and larvae sampling data from a monitoring system with a grid of points or sampling plots across seven geographic regions. The software then analyses moth captures and larvae counts from the monitoring grid and creates input maps. The knowledge base then processes these data into a new map displaying "Hazard Potential" as its output, showing areas on the grid where moth captures indicate increasing populations and where a potential for high-level outbreaks may occur and become a hazard. The Siberian Moth Outbreak Prediction Model also uses kriging to analyze sampled larvae data. The Kondakov model predicts defoliation on a single tree, so EcoSentinel/SM processes sample data, tree by tree. Then, EcoSentinel/SM uses kriging to build the map designating "Control Indicated". This provides decisionmakers with timely and useful information that helps guide their decisions about the kind and magnitude of control actions (e.g., use of environmentally sensitive biocontrols, cutting, or other forest management practices) they might take or whether to continue monitoring, based on input from the statistical analysis and map outputs of the model.

ASIAN VERSUS EUROPEAN *ENTOMOPHAGA MAIMAIGA*/GYPSY MOTH RELATIONS

Charlotte Nielsen[1], Melody Keena[2], Michael G. Milgroom[3] and Ann E. Hajek[1]

[1]Department of Entomology, Cornell University, Ithaca, NY 14853
[2]USDA Forest Service, Northeastern Research Station Hamden, CT 06514
[3]Department of Plant Pathology, Cornell University, Ithaca, NY 14853

Abstract

The European biotype of gypsy moth, *Lymantria dispar* (L.) [Lepidoptera: Lymantriidae], was introduced in the eastern United States from France in 1868 and has since become one of the most important defoliators of broadleaved trees in North America. In addition, the Asian biotype of gypsy moth has been accidentally introduced in North America several times, but so far eradication programs appear to have been successful in preventing establishment of this strain.

Entomophaga maimaiga Humber, Shimazu & Soper [Zygomycotina: Entomophthoraceae] is a naturally occurring fungal pathogen specific to gypsy moth larvae. *E. maimaiga* was originally described from Japan and is thought to be native to Asia where it causes epizootics in gypsy moth populations, suppressing outbreak populations. *E. maimaiga* was released twice in the U.S. in an effort to control gypsy moths; an isolate originating from Tokyo, Japan was released in Massachusetts in 1910-1911 and then an isolate from Ishikawa, Japan was released in New York and Virginia in 1985-1986 (Speare & Colley 1912, Hajek et al. 1995). Despite many years of intensive surveys by insect pathologists in North America, *E. maimaiga* was not observed in the field until 1989, but since then, it has spread across the distribution of gypsy moth (Andreadis & Weseloh 1990, Hajek et al. 1995). Several hypotheses for the origin and establishment of *E. maimaiga* in the U.S. have been proposed. One hypothesis proposes that the fungus originated from one of the deliberate introductions and was present at undetectable levels until 1989; another hypothesis proposes that *E. maimaiga* was successfully introduced to the U.S. by accident (see Hajek et al. 1995). However, no matter how and when *E. maimaiga* was introduced into North America it is likely that the population experienced a restriction in size (a bottleneck) resulting in reduced genetic variability compared to the source population.

The objectives for our studies were (1) to determine whether non-North American gypsy moth strains are susceptible to North American strains of *E. maimaiga*; (2) to compare the genetic diversity of North American and Asian populations of *E. maimaiga*; and (3) to determine the origin of the North American *E. maimaiga* population.

We used bioassays to assess the variability in susceptibility, measured as time to death for gypsy moth larvae challenged with *E. maimaiga*. Cross-inoculations with host strains originating from far eastern Russia, Japan, Greece and the U.S., and pathogen originating from China, far eastern Russia, Japan and the U.S. were accomplished by injecting fungal protoplasts into larvae or by subjecting larvae to showers of conidia. We found that all *E. maimaiga* isolates tested were pathogenic to all strains of *L. dispar*, regardless of the geographical origin of the fungal isolate or inoculation method; percent mortality varied between 87 % and 100%. Fungal isolates differed significantly with regard to virulence; times from inoculation to death varied between averages of 4.1 days for one of the Japanese isolates (03JP5-1-2) to 5.4 days for a Russian isolate (99RU-1-1-1). In contrast, gypsy moth strain seemed to have little effect on time to death after inoculation with *E. maimaiga*. Based on these results we therefore expect that the populations of *E. maimaiga* already present in North America would be able to help control the Asian gypsy moth if it becomes established in North America. This does not mean that introductions of Asian gypsy moth strains into North America should be ignored, since the dynamics and behavior of the Asian and North American populations are extremely different, e.g., the gypsy moth strains from Asia have a broader host range (Baranchikov 1988), shortened egg chill requirements (Keena 1996), female flight and attractions to lights that result in egg deposition on vehicles or cargo (Wallner 1996).

These attributes could influence the effectiveness of *E. maimaiga* on gypsy moth populations since it is a well-known fact that larval behavior affects the impact and dynamics of *E. maimaiga* infections (Hajek et al. 1996, Hajek 2001, Hajek et al. 2004).

We used AFLPs to assay the genetic diversity among 30 *E. maimaiga* isolates originating from seven states in the U.S., five prefectures in Japan, one province of China and one region of far eastern Russia. Among the 14 U.S. isolates, only 10 polymorphic AFLP loci were found, whereas 56 polymorphic loci were found among the 16 Asian isolates; 29 loci were polymorphic among the 12 isolates from Japan alone. Average gene diversity for the polymorphic loci was 0.223 ± 0.005 for Asia (including Japan), 0.131 ± 0.006 for Japan only, and 0.041 ± 0.004 for the US. Thus, native populations from Asia were more diverse than the U.S. populations. These results are consistent with the expectation of a population founded from a source population by a small number of individuals. Distance and parsimony analyses of AFLP data showed that the isolates from the U.S. formed one distinct clade that was not closely related to Japanese isolates collected near the Tokyo area. The closest relative to the North American isolates was the isolate released in New York State and Virginia in 1985 and 1986. However, the released isolate is in a clade distinct from the U.S. clade. These results, plus further analysis, support the hypothesis of an undocumented introduction of *E. maimaiga* into North America from Japan are the source of the current *E. maimaiga* population that is suppressing gypsy moth populations in the U.S.

References

Andreadis, T.G. & Weseloh, R.M. 1990. **Discovery of** *Entomophaga maimaiga* **in North American gypsy moth,** *Lymantria dispar.* Proc. Natl. Acad. Sci. USA 87: 2461-2465.

Baranchikov, Y.N. 1988. **Ecological basis of the evolution of host relationships in Eurasian gypsy moth populations.** In Wallner W.E., McManus, K.A. (Tech. Coord.), Proceedings, Lymantriidae: A Comparison of Features of New and Old World Tussock Moths, USDA Gen. Tech. Rep. NE-123, pp. 319-338.

Hajek, A.E. 2001. **Larval behavior in** *Lymantria dispar* **increases risk of fungal infection.** Oecologia 126: 285-291.

Hajek, A.E., Humber, R.A. & Elkinton, J.S. 1995. **The mysterious origin of** *Entomophaga maimaiga* **in North America.** Am. Entomol. 41: 31-42.

Hajek, A.E., Butler, L. Walsh, S.R.A., Perry, J.L., Silver, J.C., Hain, F.P., ODell, T.M & Smitley, D.R.1996. **Host range of the gypsy moth (Lepidoptera: Lymantriidae) pathogen** *Entomophaga maimaiga* **(Zygomyetes: Entomophthorales) in the field versus laboratory.** Environ. Entomol. 25: 709-721.

Hajek, A.E., Strazanac J.S. Wheeler, M.M. Vermeylen, F.M. Butler, L. 2004. **Persistence of the fungal pathogen** *Entomophaga maimaiga* **and its impact on native Lymantriidae.** Biol. Control 30: 466-473.

Keena, M.A. 1996. **Comparison of hatch of** *Lymantria dispar* **(Lepidoptera: Lymantriidae) eggs from Russia and the United States after exposure to different temperatures and durations of low temperature.** Ann. Entomol. Soc. Am. 89:564-572.

Speare, A.T., & Colley, R.H. 1912. **The Artificial Use of the Brown-Tail Fungus in Massachusetts, with Practical Suggestions for Private Experiment, and a Brief Note on a Fungous Disease of the Gypsy Caterpillar.** Wright & Potter, Boston. 31 pp.

Wallner, W.E. 1996. **Invasion of the tree snatchers.** American Nurseryman March 15, 1996.

INVASIVE PLANTS AFFECTING THE MANAGEMENT OF OHIO'S FORESTS

Joanne Rebbeck, Todd F. Hutchinson and Robert P. Long

Northeastern Research Station, USDA Forest Service, 359 Main Road, Delaware, OH 43015

Abstract

Introduction

Mixed oak forests dominate much of southeastern Ohio. During the mid-1800s, vast areas of forests were completely cleared of timber to supply charcoal for more than 40 local iron furnaces. The industry declined by the late 1800s and areas reverted back to forest. These current 80- to 120 year-old second-growth forests are dominated by an oak overstory while the midstory and understory are composed of shade-tolerant and fire-sensitive species such as red maple (*Acer rubrum* L.), sugar maple (*Acer saccharum* Marsh.), blackgum (*Nyssa sylvatica* Marsh.) and beech (*Fagus sylvatica* Ehrh.) (Hutchinson et al. 2003). We began studying the impact of invasive plants primarily as a result of research related to the reintroduction of fire in these forests to promote oak regeneration. Fires have been effectively suppressed in Ohio for the last 70 years or more. In western regions of the U.S., where wildfires are more intense and often catastrophic, the introduction and establishment of invasive exotics is of major concern (Brooks et al. 2004). In eastern forests, fire effects on the ability of exotics to invade forests have not been characterized.

Of the 3,000 plant species known to occur in the forests and natural areas of Ohio, about 700 species are not native (Windus and Kromer 2001). The Ohio Department of Natural Resources (ODNR) in collaboration with The Nature Conservancy generated a list of 60 invasive species threatening Ohio's natural areas. These were separated into three categories based on their invasiveness within the state: targeted, watched, and well established species. Targeted invasive species have a statewide distribution and are the most invasive and the most difficult to control. Examples from this group that could impact forested areas include garlic mustard (*Alliaria petiolata* [Bieb.] Cavara & Grande), Japanese knotweed (*Polygonum cuspidatum* Sieb. & Zucc.), amur, Japanese, morrow, and tatarian honeysuckles (*Lonicera* spp.), and multiflora rose (*Rosa multiflora* Thunb.). Watch-list species are very invasive in neighboring

states and pose a potential threat in Ohio. Generally their distribution is limited but needs to be monitored. Examples include mile-a-minute weed (*Polygonum perfoliatum* L.) and Japanese stiltgrass (*Microstegium vimineum* [Trin.] A. Camus). Well established invasives are distributed statewide or regionally within Ohio and pose a moderate to serious threat. Tree-of-heaven (*Ailanthus altissima* [Mill.] Swingle) is representative of this group.

Native to China, *Ailanthus*, was first introduced as an ornamental to Philadelphia, PA in 1784 (Hu 1979). It is a fast-growing tree that can reach 25 m in height. It is dioecious and is a prolific seed producer with up to 325,000 seeds per tree in a single growing season (Hoshovsky 1988). It is also capable of aggressive clonal spread often creating dense thickets that can out-compete native trees (Burns and Honkala 1990). While considered shade-intolerant, *Ailanthus* clonal sprouts attached to a parent tree can persist in a shaded forest understory up to 20 years (Kowarik 1995). This species is often associated with disturbed open sites such as roadsides but can also invade disturbed sites in forests, from harvested stands to canopy gaps in old-growth forests (Knapp and Canham 2000). Although the long-term effects on native tree regeneration are not known, *Ailanthus* likely has a negative effect on native vegetation, because of its highly competitive traits and production of the allelopathic compound ailanthone (Heisey 1996).

Current Research Projects

Since 1952, long-term forestry management research has been conducted at the Vinton Furnace Experimental Forest (VFEF) in Vinton County, Ohio. The 1200-acre mixed oak hardwood forest is managed by the USDA FS Northeastern Research Station and owned by MeadWestvaco. In 1958, Gustav Hall published the complete vascular flora of the VFEF (Hall 1958). At that time, non-native species were limited to open disturbed sites such as roadsides and open-fields and represented

9% of the 535 species observed. No non-natives were reported within forest stands. In 2001, a new floristic survey of the VFEF was initiated (Hutchinson and Ortt, personal communication). One objective was to document long-term changes in the non-native flora. Japanese honeysuckle (*Lonicera japonica* Thunb.) and multiflora rose appear to have naturalized within interior regions of the forest at low to medium abundance. Several new species could pose a formidable threat to forested areas including Japanese stiltgrass, tree-of-heaven, and garlic mustard. The monitoring of these exotics throughout VFEF is ongoing, and appropriate eradication measurements are implemented when necessary.

From 1995-1999, Hutchinson (2004) monitored the herbaceous layer of four study sites in southern Ohio as part of an ecosystem level assessment of the reintroduction of fire into mixed-oak forests. Exotic plans were infrequent on both burned and unburned experimental units throughout the study. Exotics made up only 3% of the 452 taxa observed and none of the 77 most commonly observed taxa were exotic.

Prescribed burning (B), thinning (T), and the combination of thinning and burning (T+B) treatments were applied to three study sites in southern Ohio in 2000-2001, as part of the national Fire and Fire Surrogates Study. At one of the sites, Tar Hollow State Forest, *Ailanthus* became established in high densities in some areas after thin and thin+burn treatments were completed. In 2003, we mapped the pre-treatment distribution of *Ailanthus* trees, quantified post-treatment *Ailanthus* seedling/sapling abundance in 5m-radius plots (N = 280), and assessed the relationship of *Ailanthus* establishment to its pre-treatment distribution, treatment type, and light availability. Prior to treatments, *Ailanthus* trees (≥8 cm dbh) were present but not abundant. In 2003, 32 trees or stumps were geolocated within the study area (Hutchinson et al. 2004). Of those 32 trees, 28 were in T+B; 3 in T and 1 in B units. Pre-treatment measurements also indicated *Ailanthus* seedlings were infrequent. By 2003, small *Ailanthus* stems (0.5 to ~3 m height) were widely distributed and abundant (96% of plots) in the T+B unit, 39% of plots in the T unit, and

only 13 % of plots in the B unit. Visual inspections of stems indicated they originated as seedling germinants during the 2001 growing season. Open sky (%) and *Ailanthus* abundance were not significantly correlated. Our results show that the pre-treatment distribution of *Ailanthus* trees was indeed the most important factor affecting patterns of its post-treatment establishment. It is also possible that the T+B treatment enhanced germination and establishment by creating higher light levels and greater forest floor disturbance. This study shows that even when present at low densities, *Ailanthus* can disperse widely and establish in high densities after forest management activities, which may in turn inhibit the regeneration of native tree species.

Cooperative Research

A cooperative agreement entitled, "Ecological restoration of hardwood forest communities following the removal and control of tree-of-heaven (*Ailanthus altissima*)" was initiated with Dr. Brian McCarthy, Department of Environmental and Plant Biology, Ohio University in 2003. Kevin Lewis, a MS student, is working with McCarthy in the development of dose response models for three herbicides (triclopyr [Garlon], glyphosate [Roundup], and imazapyr [Arsenal]) for varying stem diameters (2.5-20 cm dbh) of *Ailanthus* trees grown under forest conditions. EZject Lance System was used to inject basal stems with encapsulated herbicides. During the summer of 2004, *Ailanthus* stems were injected with imazapyr within the T+B treatment unit of the FFS study at Tar Hollow State Forest (previously described). The objective is to assess if herbicide treatments applied a growing season prior to a prescribed fire are more effective than prescribed fire alone in the control of *Ailanthus*. An experiment is also under way at Tar Hollow State Forest to determine if neighboring trees are affected when Ailanthus is stem-injected with imazapyr. Also in progress is a study to determine how natural storage conditions affect *Ailanthus* seed viability.

Dr. Glenn Matlack and graduate student Lance Glasgow, Department of Environmental and Plant Biology, Ohio University, initiated a study of exotic plants at the VFEF in 2004. Seeds of multiflora rose and Japanese stiltgrass were planted in burned and unburned plots to determine the effects of fire on germination and establishment. Also graduate student Doug Christen and Matlack are investigating the influence of different habitats (open or closed-canopy roadsides and forest gaps or closed-canopy forest interiors) on japanese stiltgrass at the VFEF.

Acknowledgments

We thank William Borovicka, David Hosack, Will Rohrig, Zach Traylor, Brad Tucker, and Kristy Tucker for field assistance in the Tar Hollow tree-of-heaven study. The Joint Fire Sciences Program provided funding for the Ohio Hills Fire and Fire Surrogate Study.

References

Brooks, M.T., D'Antonio, C.M., Richardson, D.M., Grace, J.B., Keeley, J.E., DiTomaso, J.M., Hobbs, R.J., Pellant, M., and D. Pyke. 2004. **Effects of invasive alien plants on fire regimes.** BioScience 54:677-688.

Burns, R.M., and B. H. Honkala. 1990. **Silvics of North America, Volume 2, Hardwoods.** Agriculture Handbook 654, USDA Forest Service, Washington, DC.

Hall, G. 1958. **The vascular flora of the Vinton Furnace Experimental Forest.** The Ohio Journal of Science. 58: 357-365.

Heisey, R.M. 1996. **Identification of an allelopathic compound from *Ailanthus altissima* (Simaroubaceae) and characterization of its herbicidal activity.** American Journal of Botany 83: 192-200.

Hoshovsky, M.C. 1988 **Element Stewardship Abstract for *Ailanthus altissima*.** The Nature Conservancy, Arlington, Virginia, Edition Date: 88-11-30.

Hu, S. Y. 1979. ***Ailanthus***. Arnoldia 39:29-50.

Hutchinson, T. F. 2004. **Prescribed fire effects on understory vegetation across a topographic moisture gradient in oak forests.** Dissertation. Ohio State University, Columbus, OH.

Hutchinson, T. F., J. Rebbeck, and R. P. Long. 2004. **Abundant establishment of *Ailanthus altissima* (tree-of-heaven) after restoration treatments in an upland oak forest.** Page 515. in D. Yaussy, D.M. Hix, P.C. Goebel, and R.P. Long, editors. Proceedings of the 14th Central Hardwood Conference. USDA For. Serv. Gen. Tech. Report GTR-NE-316

Hutchinson, T.F., D.L. Rubino, E.K. Sutherland, and B.C. McCarthy. 2003. **History of forests and land-use.** Pages 17-27 in E. K. Sutherland and T. F. Hutchinson, editors. Characteristics of mixed-oak forest ecosystems in southern Ohio prior to the reintroduction of fire. USDA For. Serv. Gen. Tech. Rep. GTR-NE-299.

Knapp, L.B., and C.D. Canham. 2000. **Invasion of an old-growth forest in New York by *Ailanthus altissima*: sapling growth and recruitment in canopy gaps.** Journal of the Torrey Botanical Society 127:307-315.

Kowarik, I. 1995. **Clonal growth in *Ailanthus altissima* on a natural site in West Virginia.** Journal of Vegetation Science 6:853-856.

Windus, J. and M. Kromer. 2001. **Invasive Plants of Ohio. A series of fact sheets describing the most invasive plants in Ohio's natural areas.** Ohio Department of Natural Resources, Columbus OH.

RANGE EXPANSION OF THE PINE PROCESSIONARY MOTH IN EUROPE. I-MECHANISMS UNDERLYING PPM EXPANSION IN FRANCE IN RELATION TO GLOBAL WARMING

Alain Roques[1], Jérome Rousselet[1], Christelle Robinet[1], Francis Goussard[1], and Andrea Battisti[2]

[1]National Institute of Agricultural Research (INRA), Zoologie Forestière, Ardon, BP 20619, 45166 Olivet, France
[2]Università degli Studi di Padova, DAAPV-Entomologia Agripolis - Viale dell'Università 16, 35020 Legnaro PD, Italy

Abstract

Pine processionary moth (PPM) constitutes a good model for studying the response of forest insects to global warming. PPM is a Mediterranean insect clearly expanding polewards. Its larval development occurs during winter and is therefore highly sensitive to minor changes in weather conditions. Moreover, the larvae build large white winter « nests », which could be easily surveyed by foresters to estimate the levels of infestation. PPM is the most important species of forest defoliator in southern Europe but it also impacts health of humans and pets because of its urticating hairs (dermatitis). Previous studies revealed that PPM cycle is largely controlled by winter weather conditions, the requirements for larval survival being assessed as follows: mean January minimum higher than -4 °C, annual solar radiation larger than 1800 h (to heat nests during winter), whilst lethal temperature was estimated at -16 °C. However, PPM surveys done since the 1960s using a permanent network of pine stands in France revealed a significant progression in both latitude and altitude between 1992 and 2002. This expansion seemed to coincide with a large increase in winter temperatures and in insolation as well but no clear evidence was provided for such relationships.

Therefore, an European Project entitled PROMOTH ("Global change and pine processionary moth: a new challenge for integrated pest management") was initiated since 2002 to address the following targets: (i) analysis of the genetic structuration of PPM populations in core and expanding areas using microsatellite markers; (ii) cartography and modelling of the expansion development in space and time; (iii) identify the physiological responses of the larvae to local variations in climate; and (iv) compare the parasitism in core and expanding areas.

To analyze the genetic structuration of PPM populations, larvae were sampled in more than 50 sites throughout the core and expanding areas in France. Microsatellite analysis (5 loci) did not show any isolation by distance in the core area when the flight-of-bird distances are considered. However, when the values of Fixation index (Fst) were plotted against distances circumventing Massif Central, isolation by distance was verified (Mantel test). We therefore hypothesized the existence of two corridors (northwestern and northeastern) for gene flow corresponding to different ways of expansion from the Mediterranean area, the populations still communicating by the southern Mediterranean range. In the expansion area of Paris Basin, the populations of the northern front appeared slightly but significantly divergent from these of the core area and from these of the Eastern Front, suggesting two ways for expansion in that area.

In the Paris Basin, the shift of the latitudinal front was estimated to have progressed of 86.7 km between 1972 and 2004, with a notable acceleration (55.6 km) during the last 10 years. The expansion coincided with a rapid increase in minimum winter temperature in both core and front area (+1.1 °C and + 0.9 °C, respectively). To test for larval survival potential, we used natural gradients to simulate weather conditions experienced by larvae during winter. From 2002 to 2004, larval colonies were translocated from core to front (two sites) and post-front areas (two sites) along two transects, using either two egg masses (2002) or 200 1st- instar larvae (2003- 2004) implanted per tree on 10 trees per site. A datalogger was used in each site to record the weather variables (T, RH, Isolation) on tree and into nest (probe). The same experiment was done in the French Alps to compare the survival at the altitudinal front. Under the 2002-2004 conditions, PPM larvae survived largely above the present front line in Paris Basin. In the southern Alps, PPM larvae also survived at altitudes much higher (>1800 m) than the current front line (1250 m). In two sites of the Alps, lethal temperatures were reached (-16.7 °C and -18 °C) but a few larvae survived.

Larva survival was directly related to feeding activity during the cold period (= period during which the weekly mean of minimum daily T° < 0 °C). Day temperature of the nest must be higher than 9 °C to induce feeding during the next night but feeding effectively occurs if night air temperature is higher than 0 °C. If one of these two conditions is not respected, larvae starve. We tentatively modelled the mean number of days of potential feeding for larvae and the mean number of consecutive days of larval starvation in Paris Basin for the periods 1991-1996 and 2000-2004 and showed that the second period was significantly more favourable to larval development. In the Alps, larva survival appeared to be positively correlated the mean of maximum temperatures in January, warmer conditions during 2002-2003 having favoured higher survival.

PPM expansion also depends on the flight capabilities of adults. Because they are too heavy, females usually fly only over short distances but flight mill experiments revealed some of them can fly 3 km at least, ie. more than previously considered. Pheromone trappings far above the front showed that males are patrolling 23 km at least above the front in both Paris Basin and in the Alps. In the latter situation, male flight capabilities allow gene flow between disconnected systems of Alpine valleys, and Italian and French populations are probably connected despite the Alpine barrier. In addition, a significantly fewer egg parasitism near the front probably facilitated the expansion (2-12% vs. 22-35% in core areas).

In conclusion, we can wonder whether the expansion could be unlimited with continuous warming. In other words, is PPM capable of reaching UK, Northeastern France, Germany and Central Europe? Indeed, susceptible hosts exist far above the front. Systematic plantations of pines along motorways also favour significantly the expansion, acting as relays for PPM progression. However, there seems to exist a daylength limit to expansion: daylength (and subsequent isolation) must allow effective nest heating during day to reach 9 °C. A tentative model for PPM expansion using different kinds of meteorological simulations for the next 50 years is under way.

WINTER MORTALITY IN *ADELGES TSUGAE* POPULATIONS IN 2003 AND 2004

Kathleen S. Shields[1] and Carole A. S-J. Cheah[2]

[1]USDA Forest Service, Northeastern Center for Forest Health Research, 51 Mill Pond Road, Hamden, CT 06514
[2]Connecticut Agricultural Experiment Station, Valley Laboratory, 153 Cook Hill Road, Windsor, CT 06095

The hemlock woolly adelgid (HWA), *Adelges tsugae* Annand, an exotic pest native to Asia, is a major threat to hemlock as a forest resource in eastern North America. The entire range of eastern hemlock is at risk, however cold winter temperatures might limit its continued northward spread. We assessed the mortality of HWA populations after the winters of 2002-2003 and 2003-2004, the coldest winters recorded in the Northeast in the past decade.

Between March and April 2003, we sampled HWA populations at 36 sites in NH, MA, CT, NY, PA, and NC. During a similar period in 2004 we sampled populations at 35 sites in ME, NH, MA, CT, NY, NJ, PA, MD, WV, and NC. Where possible, at least 100 HWA sistens, nymphal stage 2 or older, were examined from each of 10 trees at a site, totaling at least 1,000 HWA per site. Latitude, longitude, and elevation were recorded at each site. Highest and lowest daily temperatures for the period November 2002 through March 2003 were obtained from the National Climate Data Center for the weather station closest to each site. (Verified weather data for 2004 were not yet available.). Data were analyzed using the Spearman rank correlation test and multiple regression. Values of $P<0.05$ were considered significant.

In 2003, HWA winter mortality averaged 86.0% at 29 sites in NY and New England, 73.8% at six PA sites, and 11.2% at a NC site; highest mortality was 99.4% at a NH site. In 2004, HWA winter mortality averaged 93.6% at 17 NY and New England sites, 78.4% at seven PA sites, and 21.1% at the NC site; highest mortality was 100% at a NY site. Analysis of data from the winter of 2002-2003 indicates that mortality was positively correlated with degrees of latitude ($r=0.422$, $P=0.010$), even when the outlying NC site was excluded ($r=.371$, $P=0.028$), and negatively correlated with mean daily low temperature ($r=-0.626$, $P=0.03$). There was a slight negative correlation between percent mortality and the minimum temperature recorded at each site ($r=0.333$, $P=0.047$). The 35 sites sampled in 2004 extended over a greater part of the adelgid's current range and there was a stronger positive correlation between adelgid mortality and degrees of latitude ($r=0.590$, $P=0.0002$). Mortality was negatively correlated with degrees of longitude ($r=0.624$, $P=<0.0001$) and elevation ($r=0.395$, $P=0.0190$), but only latitude accounted for a significant amount of the variance in percent mortality ($P=0.0321$).

Although HWA populations are established in the eastern U.S. as far north as the Catskills in NY and southeastern NH and ME, existing populations are restricted to plant hardiness zone 5A (min. low of -26.5° to -28.8 °C), or warmer. Based on the high winter mortality that occurred in northern HWA populations in 2003 and 2004, we speculate that cold winter temperatures will limit the rate and extent of its northward spread.

RESTORATION OF THE AMERICAN ELM IN FORESTED LANDSCAPES

James M. Slavicek[1], Andrew Boose[2], Dan Balser[3] and Nicole Cavender[4]

[1]USDA Forest Service, 359 Main Road, Delaware, OH
[2]Metro Parks, 1069 W. Main Street, Westerville, OH
[3]Ohio Division of Natural Resources, Division of Forestry, 2045 Morse Rd. H-1, Columbus, OH
[4]The Wilds, 14000 International Road, Cumberland, OH4

The Forestry Sciences Laboratory, Northeastern Research Station, initiated a project in 2003 to restore the American elm in the state of Ohio. This effort is being carried out in partnership with the Ohio Department of Natural Resources Division of Forestry, Franklin County Metro Parks, and The Wilds. American elm tree strains with high levels of tolerance to Dutch elm disease (DED) were established in areas where the trees can naturally regenerate and spread. The process of regeneration will allow the American elm to co-evolve with the DED fungal pathogen to ensure this valuable tree species will not be lost from the American landscape. Five restoration sites have been established to date in Ohio: Mohican State Forest, Ashland County; Maumee State Forest, Henry County; Highbanks Metro Park, Delaware County; Glacier Ridge Metro Park, Union County; and The Wilds, Muskingum County.

The American elm was once widely distributed throughout the eastern United States and was a preferred tree for use along city streets and in the yards of many homeowners. The Dutch elm disease fungal pathogen *Ophiostoma ulmi* was introduced into the United States in 1930 and in the subsequent years has destroyed millions of American elm trees in the United States and Canada. By 1976 only 34 million of the estimated 77 million elms present in the urban landscape before introduction of the DED pathogen remained, and far fewer are still present today. The American elm's tall height coupled with its vase-like shape provides for a uniquely graceful tree that was a favorite tree used for planting along city streets and boulevards. The crowns of mature elms would span roadways, houses, and park recreation areas and provide the benefits of cleaner air and cooler temperatures. The American elm is one of few trees known that is capable of growing relatively well within the harsh urban environment of high summer temperatures, air pollution, and road salt present in northern latitudes.

One line of research on the American elm from the 1970s to the present focused on the identification of American elm isolates that could withstand the DED pathogen. Over 100,000 American elm trees were tested for resistance to Dutch elm disease. No trees were found that were resistant to DED; however, a few were identified that exhibited good levels of tolerance to the disease. Out of over 100,000 American elm trees screened for DED resistance, five trees were identified that exhibit the necessary levels of DED tolerance to withstand the disease. These five selections, Valley Forge, Princeton, New Harmony, R18-2, and Delaware 2, were used for the restoration effort.

The following aspects will be monitored at the restoration sites: tree growth, determination of basis for loss of planted trees, dates of first seed formation, number of regenerating trees and their distance from the planting site, incidence of DED at the restoration site in planted and seedling trees, and genetics of survivor trees.

PRODUCTION OF LdNPV IN CELL CULTURE BIOREACTORS

James M. Slavicek and J. Matt Gabler

USDA Forest Service, Northeastern Research Station, Delaware, OH

The development of bioreactor production methods for Gypchek would provide a means of production that can be scaled to a large capacity (production of 50,000 acre equivalents + per year), that is potentially at a lower cost than the current larval based production method, and would generate a product completely free of bacteria, fungi, and other viruses. The methods developed would be applicable to production of any baculovirus (e.g., TM-biocontrol, browntail moth virus) for use in insect pest control programs. We are currently focused on development of methods for production of Gypchek (LdNPV Isolate 203-Wild-type) in 3, 7, and 14 liter cell culture bioreactors. Briefly, the production process entails the preparation and addition of insect cell culture medium into the bioreactor. The medium is sterilized by filtration as the medium is pumped in the bioreactor. Ld652Y cells are then added that were grown to the proper density in a shake flask. Once the cells reach the appropriate density, budded virus is added to begin the infection process. Polyhedra are isolated by centrifugation at the end of a production run. The final product is nearly pure polyhedra, and lacks bacterial, viral, and fungal contaminants. Recent studies have focused on determination of the maximal cell density that can be achieved, analysis of spent media, and determination of the optimal ratio of budded virus:host cells to use for production of polyhedra. The amount of polyhedra produced in bioreactors is dependent upon the number of cells present. Maximum polyhedra production will be achieved when an infection is performed using the maximum possible number of cells per liter of medium. To determine the maximum density to which Ld652Y cells can be grown, cells were seeded into the 2 and 5 liter bioreactors and grown until cell growth nearly stopped. A cell density of approximately 1×10^7 cells/ml was achieved, when using an agitation speed of 75 rpm and a dissolved oxygen concentration of 50% of saturation. Depletion of a medium component, such as glucose or an amino acid, during the cell growth phase of polyhedra production could cause cell growth to stop and hence negatively impact polyhedra production. An analysis of medium was performed after a cell density of about 1×10^7 cells/ml was achieved. No amino acid, vitamin, or glucose was found to be depleted. A high utilization of aspartic acid, glutamine, tyrosine, and serine was found. From 27% to 38% of the starting amount of these amino acids were utilized during the cell growth phase. Approximately 54% of the riboflavin present was used. Cholesterol may be limiting cell growth since it was depleted from the medium. There was no build up of the metabolic byproducts ammonia and lactate that are generated by the metabolism of glutamine and glucose, respectively. These byproducts can be inhibitory to cell growth if their levels become too high. Polyhedra production was found to be significantly greater when using a multiplicity of infection (m.o.i.) of 0.005 virus particles per cell compared to using a m.o.i. of 0.01. Polyhedra production levels of 4.8×10^{11} and 5.8×10^{11} polyhedra per liter have been achieved to date in the 2 and 5 liter bioreactors, respectively. Preliminary results suggest that the sparging rate and cell growth rate can impact polyhedra production. These parameters are under investigation.

DOES COMMUNITY STRUCTURE INFLUENCE FOREST SUSCEPTIBILITY AND RESPONSE TO EMERALD ASH BORER?

Annemarie Smith[1], Daniel A. Herms[2] and Robert P. Long[3]

[1]The Ohio State University, Environmental Science Graduate Program, 400 Aronoff Laboratory, 318 W. 12th Street, Columbus, Ohio 43210
[2]Department of Entomology, The Ohio State University, Ohio Agricultural Research and Development Center, 1680 Madison Avenue, Wooster, OH 44691
[3]USDA Forest Service, 359 Main Road, Delaware, OH 43015

Abstract

Emerald ash borer (*Agrilus planipennis* Fairmaire) (EAB) is an exotic, invasive beetle that has infested and killed more than 12 million ash trees (*Fraxinus* species) in southeastern Michigan. If not contained and eradicated, EAB has the potential to devastate ash throughout North America with substantial economic and ecological consequences. The objectives of this research are to (1) determine effects of community composition and stand structure on forest susceptibility to EAB invasion; and (2) quantify effects of EAB-induced ash mortality on forest community composition. In 11 stands studied in southeast Michigan in 2004, there was no relationship between ash density or relative dominance of ash and EAB-induced dieback, which was high in all stands. *Ulmus* (elm), *Acer* (maple) and *Prunus* (cherry) were the most common non-host species in the understory, suggesting that they will replace ash in the canopy layer, at least in the short term. Ash, however, was the most common species in the sapling and seedling layers, and thus will provide a continual supply of host material for EAB, which will complicate eradication efforts. The EAB invasion has the potential eliminate ash from hardwood forests and alter the composition of North American forest communities.

HOST SPECIFICITY OF GYPSY MOTH MICROSPORIDIA: FIELD STUDIES IN SLOVAKIA

L. Solter[1], D. Pilarska[2], M. McManus[3], J. Novotny[4], M. Zubrik[4], J. Patocka[4]*

[1]Illinois Natural History Survey, 607 E. Peabody Dr., Urbana, IL 61801, USA
[2]Bulgarian Academy of Sciences, 1 Tsar Osvoboditel, Sofia 1000, Bulgaria
[3]USDA Forest Service, NE Research Station, 51 Mill Pond Rd., Hamden, CT 06514, USA
[4]Forest Research Institute, Lesnicka 11, 96900 Banska Stiavnica, Slovak Republik, *Affiliate

Three genera of microsporidia, *Endoreticulatus* (*schubergi*), *Nosema* spp., and *Vairimorpha* sp., infect gypsy moth (*Lymantria dispar* (L.)) larval populations and have been documented to reduce the intensity and duration of gypsy moth outbreaks in Europe. In order to satisfy regulatory protocols for introducing isolates of these pathogens into North American gypsy moth populations as classical biological control agents, host specificity issues must be addressed. Previous laboratory studies indicateed that native North American Lepidoptera that are forest foliage feeders have a broad range of susceptibility to gypsy moth microsporidia and that *Endoreticulatus* has the broadest host range. Neither atypical infections nor host-like infections of *Nosema* and *Vairimorpha* were horizontally or vertically transmitted between infected and uninfected conspecific nontarget individuals. Field studies in Bulgaria determined that other lepidopteran species did not serve as natural reservoirs for the gypsy moth microsporidia in the native areas.

We are currently evaluating the effects of microsporidia on field populations of nontarget Lepidoptera when introduced via ultra low volume sprays as a worst case scenario. One and two weeks after ground application of 1 billion spores per plot (5 x 10^5 spores/ml), over 70 species of lepidopteran larvae were collected from the sprayed oak trees, identified to species and dissected to recover any microsporidia present. Of nine nontarget species infected with *Vairimorpha*-like microsporidia, four were infective to the gypsy moth. The other isolates did not infect gypsy moth. As predicted by laboratory studies, six species with *Vairimorpha*-like infections were noctuids (four *Orthosia* spp.), and one lymantriid, *Orgyia antigua*, was susceptible. Although geometrid species are typically refractive, one of 16 species recovered was infected with *Vairimorpha*; however, this isolate was not infective to gypsy moth. The plots sprayed with *Vairimorpha* sp. in 2002 were monitored for the following 2 years and no new *Vairimorpha* infections were recovered. *Nosema*-like isolates were recovered from three nontarget species in two seasons of spraying/collecting. None of these isolates were infective to third instar gypsy moth larvae, nor did spore morphology suggest that they were gypsy moth isolates. Dosages of *Nosema* for the final 2005 season will be quadrupled to increase the prevalence of infection of gypsy moth larvae used as positive controls, and to increase the probability of identifying any and all susceptible nontarget hosts.

THE FIRST NATURAL ENEMIES OF EMERALD ASH BORER FOUND IN CHINA

John S. Strazanac[1] and Yang Zhong-qi[2]

[1]West Virginia University, Morgantown, WV
[2]Research Institute of Forest Protection, Chinese Academy of Forestry, Beijing, P.R. China

The first two parasitoids reported to be reared from the emerald ash borer (EAB), *Agrilus planipennis* Fairmaire, in its native range of China have potential to be useful in biocontrol efforts in North America. Both feed gregariously upon the larvae of EAB in their galleries and have multiple generations each season. One is a member of the genus *Spathius* (Braconidae: Doryctinae), a group specializing on bark and wood boring beetle larvae. The other belongs to the genus *Tetrastichus* (Eulophidae), a highly speciose group with members known to attack Coleoptera, other Hymenoptera, Diptera and Lepidoptera. Illustrations are provided and their basic biology described including life histories and ovipositional behavior described.

EFFECTS OF GYPSY MOTH POPULATION DENSITY AND HOST-TREE SPECIES ON PARASITISM

Lidia Sukovata[1] and Roger W. Fuester[2]

[1]Forest Research Institute, 3 Bitwy Warszawskiej 1920 St., 00-973 Warsaw, Poland
[2]USDA ARS Beneficial Insects Introduction Research Unit, 501 South Chapel St., Newark, DE 19713-3814

Abstract

The gypsy moth (*Lymantria dispar* L.) is a defoliator of deciduous forests throughout most of Eurasia and the northeastern part of the USA. In Poland, the economic importance of the gypsy moth is rather low. Sporadically it causes local outbreaks, which are suppressed by a complex of natural enemies, mostly virus and parasitoids. These studies were conducted in 2003 and 2004 in the Biebrza National Park located in the northeastern Poland.

The research was conducted at three sites characterized as follows: Kopciowe (sparse gypsy moth population in both years), Barwik (outbreak in 2003 and post-outbreak in 2004), and Honczarowska (outbreak in 2004). At Kopciowe, we used trap larvae that were reared in the laboratory from egg masses collected in the field and exposed 3-4 times during the season on oak saplings placed in 3-5 cages covered with netting. At Barwik and Honczarowska, gypsy moth larvae were sampled 4-5 times during the season from 4-5 species of trees (40-50 larvae/tree species/site): *Alnus glutinosa*, *Salix cinerea* (only at Barwik), *Betula* spp., *Quercus robur* and *Corylus avellana*. Larvae collected were reared individually on fresh oak leaves in plastic cups.

Parasitism at Barwik was up to 45% in 2003, but decreased to 35% in 2004. In the outbreak phase the co-dominant parasitoid species were *Blepharipa* spp. (up to 35%) and *Parasetigena silvesris* (up to 9%), whereas in the post-outbreak phase, *P. silvestris* was more efficient (24% max. peak parasitism) than *Blepharipa* spp. (13% max. peak parasitism). At Honczarowska, the total parasitism in 2004 reached 68%, due mostly to *P. silvestris* which parasitized 53% of the larvae. *Blepharipa* spp. (*schineri* and *pratensis*) were subdominant (up to 19.8% parasitism). In the sparse population, total parasitism was up to 39% in 2003 and 48% in 2004. The dominant parasitoid species were *Compsilura concinnata* (up to 31.8%) in 2003 and *Aphantorhaphopsis samarensis* (up to 43%) in 2004. The results of 2-year studies showed no consistent relationship between gypsy moth parasitism by *Blepharipa* spp. and *P. silvestris* and the tree species from which host larvae were collected. In 2003, parasitism by both species was higher on *Alnus* and *Betula* than on *Salix*, but in 2004, parasitization by *Blepharipa* was highest on *Salix*, which had the highest gypsy moth density and concomitant defoliation, but parasitism by *P. silvestris* was lowest on the same host plant, suggesting that defoliation can also be a determinant of parasitism.

WEEDUS: DATABASE OF PLANTS INVADING NATURAL AREAS IN THE UNITED STATES

Jil M. Swearingen

National Park Service, Center for Urban Ecology, 4598 MacArthur Blvd., N.W., Washington, DC 20007

WeedUS may provide the most current and comprehensive compilation of invasive plant species affecting natural ecosystems that is currently available. Over 1,000 plant species that have been reported to be invading natural areas in the U.S., including Hawaii, have been entered into the WeedUS database as of November 2004. Additional species are undergoing review to determine or clarify native origin, natural range, taxonomic status, etc. before being included. Requirements for inclusion in the database are that the plant be exhibiting invasive behavior in a "natural area", generally excluding intensively managed lands such as croplands and forestry plantations. Reports of additional invasive plant species and occurrences are welcome and will be added to the database as received.

Data for WeedUS are based on the observations and expert opinions of botanists, ecologists, invasive species specialists, and other professionals. Information is derived from a wide variety of sources (N=130) including publications, reports, surveys, and personal observations. Sources include the National Park Service (59 units), other federal, state, and local agencies, Exotic Pest Plant Councils and sister organizations, The Nature Conservancy, universities, and others. Database fields include genus; species; author; synonyms (selected); common name; family; plant habit(s); native origin; U.S. nativity; states, national parks, and regions where reported invasive; federal noxious weed status; and source references. For consistency, taxonomy follows Kartesz (1999).

Some applications of the database include: 1) state and regional level occurrence information for use in mapping occurrences of ecologically important invasive plants; 2) improved predictive abilities for potential spread; 3) improved invasive species prevention and management abilities; 4) baseline data for invasive plant ranking and prioritization; and 5) identification of information and research gaps.

A subset of the WeedUS database (common name, scientific name, states and national parks where invasive, and references), is posted to the Plant Conservation Alliance, Alien Plant Working Group web page "Weeds Gone Wild: Alien Plant Invaders of Natural Areas" at http://www.nps.gov.plants/alien. Publication of the full WeedUS database is currently being investigated.[1]

---

[1]The Plant Conservation Alliance was initially established by a Memorandum of Agreement signed by ten federal agencies in May 1994. It is also supported by many non-federal Cooperators, currently numbering over 200.

PARASITISM OF THE BROWN SPRUCE LONGHORN BEETLE, *TETROPIUM FUSCUM* (FABR.) (COLEOPTERA: CERAMBYCIDAE) IN HALIFAX, NOVA SCOTIA.

J. Sweeney[1], J. Price[1], S. Sopow[1], G. Smith[1], Gavin Broad[2] and Henri Goulet[3]

[1]Natural Resources Canada, Canadian Forest Service, PO Box 4000, Fredericton, NB, E3B 5P7
[2]Biological Records Centre, Centre for Ecology & Hydrology, Monks Wood, Cambs, England PE28 2LS
[3]Agriculture and AgriFood Canada, Eastern Cereal and Oilseed Research Centre, 960 Carling Ave. Ottawa, ON K1A 0C6

Abstract

The brown spruce longhorn beetle, *Tetropium fuscum* (Fabr.), native to Europe and established near Halifax, NS, since at least 1990, is currently the target of a survey and eradication program. *Tetropium fuscum* is host to several species of parasitoids in Europe. In the event that eradication is not successful, biological control may provide an option for long term management of *T. fuscum.* Our objectives were to determine the incidence of parasitism of *T. fuscum* in the Halifax population, and the identity and origin of parasitoid species. Bait logs of red spruce, *Picea rubens* Sarg., were set out in Point Pleasant Park and other sites in the Halifax area in May of 2000, 2001 and 2002. In late fall-early winter, the logs were either sawn into 1 cm thick slabs to isolate individual *Tetropium* larvae, or cut into 35 cm long bolts. Bolts and slabs were incubated at 21 °C for 12 weeks and the number and species of adult *Tetropium* spp. and parasitoids recorded. Two Nearctic hymenoptera species were found commonly parasitizing *T. fuscum* and the native North American species, *Tetropium cinnamopterum* (L.): *Rhimphoctona macrocephala* (Prov.) (Hymenoptera: Ichneumonidae) and *Wroughtonia occidentalis* Cresson (Hymenoptera: Braconidae). Positive host-parasitoid associations were made by isolating individual *Tetropium* prepupae in red spruce slabs and identifying the species as either *T. fuscum* or *T. cinnamopterum* using distinctive morphological features (Smith and Gill, unpublished). Subsequent adult examinations confirmed the species identity of all prepupae that successfully completed development. Of 25 prepupae identified as *T. fuscum*, there emerged 18 *T. fuscum* adults, 4 *Rhimphoctona macrocephala* (Provancher) and 3 *Wroughtonia occidentalis* (Cresson). Of 29 prepupae identified as *T. cinnamopterum*, there emerged 23 *T. cinnamopterum* adults, 3 *R. macrocephala*, and 3 *W. occidentalis*. Percent parasitism of *Tetropium* spp. ranged from 0-25% for *R. macrocephala* and from 5-56% for *W. occidentalis*. *Rhimphoctona macrocephala* and *W. occidentalis* are koinobionts, i.e., the host development continues after parasite oviposition. Each parasitoid species emerges from the host prepupa and forms a cocoon within the pupal chamber. To our knowledge, these are the first records of parasitism of *T. fuscum* by Nearctic parasitoids. With greater knowledge of the factors affecting parasitoid foraging and survival, it may be possible to enhance their impact on *T. fuscum* in Nova Scotia.

BEAUVERIA BASSIANA FOR CONTROL OF THE BROWN SPRUCE LONGHORN BEETLE, *TETROPIUM FUSCUM* (FABR.) (COLEOPTERA: CERAMBYCIDAE).

J. Sweeney[1], G. Thurston[1], R. Lavallée[2], R. Trudel[3], P. Desrochers[2], C. Côté[2], C. Guertin[3], S. Todorova[3], H.H. Kope[4] and R. Alfaro[4]

[1]Natural Resources Canada, Canadian Forest Service (NRCAN-CFS), PO Box 4000, Fredericton, NB, E3B 5P7 (jsweeney@nrcan.gc.ca)
[2]NRCAN-CFS, Laurentian Forestry Centre, Quebec, QC
[3]INRS - Institut Armand-Frappier, Laval, QC
[4]NRCAN-CFS, Pacific Forestry Centre, Victoria, BC

Abstract

Beauveria bassiana is a soil-borne fungus that occurs naturally throughout the world and infects a wide variety of insects but is not toxic to mammals, birds, or plants. *Beauveria*-based pest control products are commercially available in the U.S. and other parts of the world, but not Canada. We are investigating *B. bassiana* as a means of suppressing populations of the brown spruce longhorn beetle, *Tetropium fuscum* (Fabr.), an exotic wood boring beetle discovered in Halifax, Nova Scotia, in 1999. In laboratory bioassays, adult *Tetropium* spp. were susceptible to *B. bassiana* isolates from both Quebec and Nova Scotia. Field trials were conducted in 2004 to test the efficacy of *B. bassiana* for infecting foraging adult beetles. Two methods were used to infect foraging adult *T. fuscum*: 1) polyester bands impregnated with *B. bassiana* conidospores wrapped around the stems of live spruce trees; and 2) application of concentrated conidiospore suspensions directly to spruce bait logs once per week for four weeks during the peak flight season (June). The tree bands captured 24 *T. fuscum* and 93 nontarget beetle species. Percent infection of pooled beetle species (*T. fuscum* plus nontarget species) was significantly greater on treated bands (37%) than untreated bands (7%); percent infection of *T. fuscum* was not significantly greater on treated bands (67%) than on untreated bands (33%), likely due to the small total (n=24) captured. Application of *B. bassiana* to the spruce logs did not significantly suppress brood production in the logs: the mean number of *T. fuscum* pupal cells per 1 m log did not differ between untreated logs (7.4) and logs treated with *B. bassiana* isolates from Quebec (6.8) or Nova Scotia (2.5). Our results indicate that *T. fuscum* is susceptible to *B. bassiana* under field conditions and that tree bands, and not bait log applications, may be a better strategy for further tests.

THE INFLUENCE OF STAND THINNING ON SURROGATE PHEROMONE PLUMES

Harold W. Thistle[1], Holly Peterson[2], Gene Allwine[3], Brian Lamb[3], Steve Edburg[3] and Brian Strom[4]

[1]USDA Forest Service, FHTET, 180 Canfield St., Morgantown, WV 26505
[2]Montana Technical University, Department of Environmental Engineering, 1300 West Park, Butte, MT 59701
[3]Washington State University, Department of Civil and Environmental Engineering, Pullman, WA 99164-3140
[4]USDA Forest Service, Southern Research Station, Pineville, LA 71360

Abstract

The objective of this study is to determine how stand density affects the behavior of pheromone plumes in a southern pine stand. Thinning is known to reduce southern pine beetle (SPB, *Dendroctonus frontalis* Zimmermann) mortality in southern pine stands (Lorio, 1980). The mechanisms by which this occurs are not yet clear but probably consist of multiple, perhaps even synergistic, factors. It is possible that changes in the dispersion and physical movement of pheromone plumes in these stands as they are thinned impacts the risk of infestation. Also, the effectiveness of pheromone management strategies may be improved by determining the spacing and location of pheromone dispensers in the trunk space of a forest stand so that plume dispersal and shape can be optimized. In more generic terms, this data set will compliment previous work (Thistle et al. 2004) in an effort to develop in-stand dispersion models and analytical techniques that will allow pest managers to optimize placement and location in the development of in-stand pest control strategies. In the past few decades, outbreaks of North American bark beetles have brought about renewed interest in these often devastating forest pests. The impact of these outbreaks and the anticipated impact of future outbreaks have stimulated the continuation of basic and applied research on the use of semiochemicals to manipulate bark beetle populations (Werner and Holsten 1995). In the southern U. S., losses to SPB are often dramatic and have reached unprecedented proportions in recent years (USDA Forest Service 2003). To mitigate forest losses and improve forest health, initiatives emphasizing thinning pine stands have recently been funded.

The method used here is a tracer experiment utilizing SF_6 and 30 min mean samplers described in Krasnec et al. (1984) combined with high frequency sampling described in Benner and Lamb (1985). The basic configuration (Thistle et al. 1995, Thistle et al. 2004) is to surround a point source of SF_6 with a dense array of mean samplers. A high frequency sampler is deployed at one point on the mean array so the structure of the plume at high frequency can be compared to the mean plume. SF_6 is chosen because it can be detected at concentrations as low as 10 ppt (even at 1 Hz), is conservative (fairly non-reactive in the environment) and a large body of scientific literature exists utilizing it as a gaseous tracer.

These tests were run on the Winn Ranger District of the Kisatchie National Forest outside of Winnfield, LA. The basic array consisted of 50, 30-minute mean SF_6 samplers, a 7 port sampler collecting 5 minute mean SF_6 samples and one high frequency sampler collecting 1 Hz data. Fourteen trial days were run. Each trial consisted of 4.5 hours of data or nine, 30-minute samples collected sequentially. When all the samplers are considered, this renders around 450 30-minute samples per test along with the 5-minute and 1 Hz records. The samplers are arrayed in concentric circles around the source. The canopy on the site was a loblolly pine canopy with a dense understory. Four trials were run in the unthinned canopy, then the understory was removed and three trials were run in the canopy with a basal area of about 140 ft[2], three trials were then run with the canopy thinned to a basal area of 100 ft[2] and finally four trials were run with the basal area reduced to 70 ft[2].

Data analysis has only begun but the two graphs below are enlightening. In the first time series (Figure 1), the plume passages past the single, 1 Hz sampling point show a large degree of coherence and multiple peaks in each plume passage. This is a low wind speed, low dispersion, atmospherically stable environment. The plume moves laterally slowly so that the time series shows extended periods of SF_6 at the sampler port. The plume is meandering back and forth over a small range giving multiple peaks at the port as the plume

15 May 2004
13:00 through 13:30
10-m arc - 120 deg

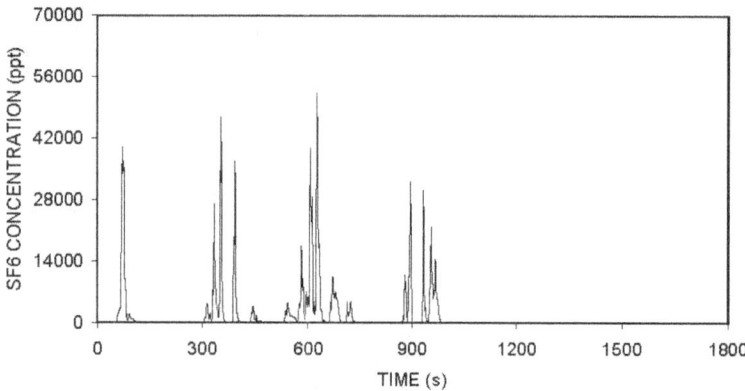

Figure 1.—Time series of SF$_6$ collected on the 10 m arc in the unthinned loblolly pine canopy.

27 May 2004
07:30 through 08:00
5-m arc - 90 deg

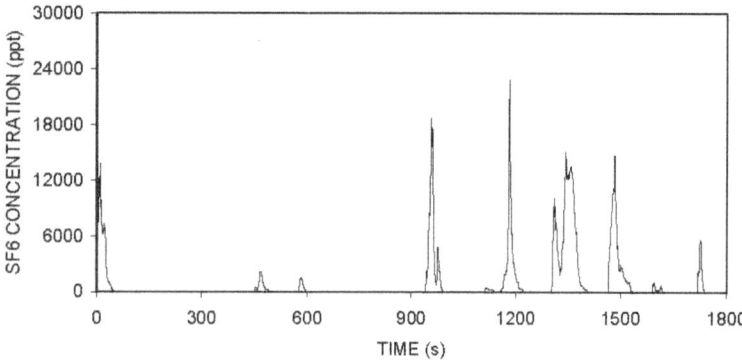

Figure 2.—Time series of SF$_6$ collected on the 5 m arc in the loblolly pine canopy thinned to 70 ft^2 basal area.

centerline meanders back and forth across it. This then contrasts with Figure 2 measured in the canopy with basal area of 70 ft^2 allowing a much more energetic flow regime to penetrate into the canopy. The floor of the canopy receives direct solar radiation so the canopy is atmospherically unstable. The larger turbulent scales associated with this flow regime are expressed in the time series which consists of more discrete peaks as the plume meanders across a wider range and crosses the single point less often leaving a larger number of zeroes in the series between plume crossings. (For discussion of similar plume structures measured or inferred in pheromone research the reader is referred to Aylor et al. 1976, Murlis and Jones 1981, Elkinton et al. 1984 and Mafra-Neto and Carde 1994.)

The implications of these data are not presently clear but thinning does have a dramatic influence on ventilation, incident solar radiation and the dispersive characteristics of the in-canopy environment. Plumes in the less dense canopy will have a larger meander range which may increase the probability of encounter by an insect but the higher velocity flows and increased wander of the plumes probably causes them to be ripped apart by the trees thus rendering them less coherent and difficult to associate with the point source where they originated. The plumes in the thicker canopies exist in a low dispersion environment and may be easier to track though they are not moving away from the point source as quickly. It is expected, however, that they will remain more concentrated for a longer distance in the stable trunk space atmosphere although they will move more slowly due to the very low velocity ambient flows.

References

Aylor, D., J. Parlange, and J. Granett. 1976. **Turbulent dispersion of disparlure in the forest and male gypsy moth response.** Environ. Ent. 5: 1026-1032.

Benner, R.L., and B. Lamb. 1985. **A fast response continuous analyzer for halogenated atmospheric tracers.** J. Atmos. Ocean Tech. 2: 582-589.

Elkinton, J., R. Carde, and C. Mason. 1984. **Evaluation of time-average dispersion models for estimating pheromone concentration in a deciduous forest.** J. Chem. Ecol. 10: 1081-1108.

Krasnec, J., D. Demaray, B. Lamb, and R. Benner. 1984. **Automated sequential syringe sampler for atmospheric tracer studies.** J. Atmos. Ocean. Tech. 1: 372-378.

Lorio, P.L., Jr. 1980. **Loblolly pine stocking levels affect potential for southern pine beetle infestations.** Southern Journal of Applied Forestry. 4: 162-165.

Mafra-Neto, A., and R.T. Carde. 1994. **Fine-scale structure of pheromone plume modulates upwind orientation of flying moths.** Nature 369: 142-144.

Murlis, J., and C. Jones. 1981. **Fine scale structure of odour plumes in relation to insect orientation to distance pheromone and other attractant sources.** Physiol. Entomol. 6: 71-86.

Thistle, H.W., D.R. Murray, M.R. Ratte, and M.R. Carroll. 1995. **Atmospheric Tracer Concentrations from an Elevated Source in Urban Core.** J. of Env. Engineering, Vol. 121(l): 5-15 January

Thistle H.W., H. Peterson, G. Allwine, B. Lamb, T. Strand, E.H. Holsten and P.J. Shea. 2004. **Surrogate Pheromone Plumes in Three Forest Trunk Spaces: Composite Statistics and Case Studies.** Forest Science, 50(5) pp. 610-625.

U.S.D.A. Forest Service. 2003. **Forest insect and disease conditions in the United States 2002.** USDA Forest Service Forest Health Protection Washington, D.C. June 2003. 124 pp.

Werner, R.A., and E.H. Holsten. 1995. **Current status of research with the spruce beetle, *Dendroctonus rufipennis*.** P. 23-29 *in* Proc. of the National Entomological Society of America meeting: Application of semiochemicals for management of bark beetle infestations, Salom, S.M., and K.R. Hobson (eds.). USDA For. Serv. Gen. Tech. Rep. INT-GTR-318.

PERSISTENCE OF INVADING GYPSY MOTH POPULATIONS

Patrick C. Tobin[1] and Stefanie L. Whitmire[2]

[1]USDA Forest Service, Northeastern Research Station, 180 Canfield Street, Morgantown, WV 26505
(304) 285-1514 (Bus.); (304) 285-1505 (Fax), ptobin@fs.fed.us
[2]West Virginia University, Department of Biology, P.O. Box 6057, Morgantown, WV 26506, whitmir3@msu.edu

Abstract

Exotic invasive species are a mounting threat to native biodiversity, and their direct and indirect effects are gaining increasingly more attention at each detection. Equally important are the dynamics of those exotic invasives that are already well established and for whom eradication is no longer possible. While the literature reports many examples of the ability of a newly arrived exotic invader to persist prior to detection and population growth, we focused on the persistence dynamics of an established invader using the European gypsy moth in North America as a model system. The spread of gypsy moth is largely thought to be the result of the growth and coalescence of isolated colonies ahead of the generally infested area. One important question is thus the ability of these isolated colonies to persist when subject to Allee effects and/or inimical stochastic events. We used U.S. gypsy moth survey data, collected from pheromone-baited traps, to examine persistence of gypsy moth colonies within (1) the transition zone, which extends from Wisconsin to Virginia; and (2) an designated uninfested area along the North Shore, Minnesota.

Within the transition zone of gypsy moth, which is the area between the generally infested and uninfested areas, we used Local Indicator of Spatial Autocorrelation methods. This novel spatial statistical tool was used to objectively identify isolated colonies of gypsy moth from pheromone-baited traps deployed under the Slow-the-Spread project. We then determined region-specific probabilities of colony persistence given the population abundance in the previous year and its relationship to a suite of ecological factors. We observed that colonies in Wisconsin were significantly more likely to persist in the following year than in other geographic regions of the transition zone. Moreover, across all regions, the abundance of preferred host tree species and land use category did not appear to influence persistence. The enhanced rates of persistence in Wisconsin may help explain the more rapid rate of spread in this region, and

motivates important questions regarding the management of established exotics as they invade new areas.

In the North Shore of Minnesota, pheromone-baited traps are used in detection, and space-time data from 2000-2004 were available. Analysis of detection data, particularly for newly arrived exotic invasive species, is complex. In most cases, distributions are not only overwhelming dominated by zeros, but also the majority of counts exceeding 0 are more often than not one. Thus, the distribution is not only highly skewed, but often quite close to binary. One approach to overcoming these issues in invasive species ecology is to consider methods used in the epidemiological community, in which disease incidence can be rare and binary, and many of the underlying objectives are not dissimilar. In an epidemiological context, the focus is to quickly detect space-time clustering of disease prevalence so that potential outbreaks are minimized and epidemics avoided. In invasive species population biology, a similar desire for an early warning system exists so that new invaders can be aggressively addressed prior to population expansion. In our case, the primary goal of an analysis of the North Shore data was to determine if male moths were being trapped at the same place over time, or if they were random in space and time. In other words, do the data suggest the presence of reproducing populations established at low abundance, stochastic introductions from year to year, or some combination of both? We used the Knox test, a common tool in epidemiology, to quantify the space-time signature of the North Shore data, and compared it to a series of simulated data from a (1) random space-time pattern; (2) deterministic space-time clustered pattern; and (3) stochastic model that allowed random introductions and extinctions in each year, as well as stochastic nearest neighbor dispersal of existing colonies. The preliminary results suggest that the North Shore contains a complex mix of established colonies with random introductions and extinctions to some yet unknown degree. The next step in this analysis is to partition and quantify these processes.

A NOVEL ELASTASE-LIKE PROTEIN FROM THE GYPSY MOTH IS INVOLVED IN THE PROTEOLYTIC ACTIVATION OF *BACILLUS THURINGIENSIS* TOXINS

Algimantas P. Valaitis

USDA Forest Service, Delaware OH 43015

Abstract

Crystal proteins (Cry) from the bacterium *Bacillus thuringiensis* (Bt) are known for their insecticidal activity. The most widely used Bt-based bioinsecticides in agriculture and forestry in North America are based on the HD-1 isolate of *B. thuringiensis* subsp. *kurstaki*, which produces three distinct insecticidal proteins called Cry1Aa, Cry1Ab and Cry1Ac. After ingestion by susceptible insects, the crystals are solubilized in the alkaline environment of the midgut; protoxins with an apparent size of 130-140 kDa are released and proteolytically processed by midgut proteases, producing activated toxins with an apparent size of 55-60 kDa. The activated toxins bind to specific receptors on the midgut epithelium membrane. An additional proteolytic cleavage of the toxins is believed to be a prerequisite for insertion of the toxins into the membrane and for pore formation.

In this study, an elastase-like protease with an apparent size of 50 kDa that binds Cry1A toxins was found in gypsy moth larval digestive fluids. The protein was purified by a calcium precipitation step followed by ion-exchange and gel filtration chromatography. In contrast to gypsy moth trypsin and chymotrypsin, the elastase-like protease interacts with the calcium-mimic dye Stains-all and is recognized by antibodies raised to the putative Bt toxin receptor (BTR-270) purified from gypsy moth brush border membrane vesicles. The digestion of Cry1A protoxin using purified gypsy moth trypsin, chymotrypsin, and elastase generates products that are different in size, suggesting that the activities of these products may be different. In addition, the elastase-like protease binds trypsin-activated Cry1A toxin and produces an activated toxin smaller than trypsin or chymotrypsin, implying that it may be involved in the final step of activation of the Bt toxin, which triggers formation of a membrane-competent pre-pore structure necessary for insertion of the Bt toxin into the membrane and for toxicity.

INVESTIGATING THE ROLE OF THE CADHERIN-LIKE PROTEIN FROM GYPSY MOTH AS A *BACILLUS THURINGIENSIS* CRY1A TOXIN RECEPTOR

Algimantas P. Valaitis[1], Karen J. Garner[1], Juan L. Jurat-Fuentes[2] and Michael J. Adang[2,3]

[1]USDA Forest Service, Delaware, OH 4301

Departments of [2]Entomology and [3]Molecular Biology, University of Georgia, Athens, Georgia 30602

Abstract

Bacillus thuringiensis (Bt) crystal proteins are pore-forming toxins which have been used for over 40 years as an alternative to chemical pesticides. Due to environmental and health concerns, there has been a major increase in the proportion of areas in North America treated with Bt at the expense of chemical insecticides, and this trend is expected to continue. As an insecticide, Bt is valued for its low developmental cost and its specificity. Although more than 3,000 insects from 16 orders are susceptible to Bt toxins, only a limited number of Bt toxins are highly effective against important forest and agricultural insect pests. Additional limitations, including the resistance to Bt in older larvae justify the search for approaches to develop new Bt-based products with increased insecticidal activity and specificity towards target insect pests.

The specificity of Bt Cry1Aa toxins is mainly determined by the presence of specific midgut receptors in susceptible target insects. Cadherin-like proteins from several insect species have been demonstrated to function as Cry1A toxin receptors when expressed in non-susceptible insect cell lines. Thus, a cDNA encoding a homolog of these cadherins (LdCad) from the gypsy moth, *Lymantria dispar*, was cloned and inserted into an expression vector to construct a system that displays LdCad on the surface of *Drosophila* S2 cells. Expression of LdCad was detected using antibodies raised to a short amino acid region of the cadherin protein from *Heliothis virescens*. Current efforts are concentrated on testing Cry1A toxin binding and cytotoxicity towards S2 cells expressing LdCad. Development of a functional cell-based assay system for exploiting the gypsy moth Bt receptor will be valuable for identifying key residues involved in toxin recognition and for designing new toxins with increased effectiveness and specificity towards gypsy moth.

HOST RANGE OF *ANOPLOPHORA GLABRIPENNIS*: WHAT WE'VE LEARNED FROM COMMON-GARDEN EXPERIMENT DATA

Baode Wang[1], Vic Mastro[1], and Ruitong Gao[2]

[1] USDA-APHIS-PPQ-PSDEL, Bldg. 1398, Otis ANGB, MA 02542
[2] Research Institute of Forest Ecology, Environment, and Protection, Chinese Academy of Forestry

A "common garden" experiment was conducted at two sites in China to test preference of the Asian longhorned beetle (ALB), *Anoplophora glabripennis* to important tree species, especially trees from different families whose status as a host was not clear. Parameters relevant to preference of host: feeding, oviposition, and suitability for development were evaluated.

The selection of tree species was primarily based on the distributional and economic importance of tree species in the U.S. and in China. The results of earlier tests conducted in the Otis laboratory in 1997-1998 were also taken into the consideration. Other factors such as information contained in literature and the survey results from the New York and Chicago infestations, also contributed to the selection of test species. Trees (40-60 from each of the 25 selected species) primarily from China were planted in one site in northwestern China, while trees from the U. S. (40 from each of the 20 selected species) were planted in Beijing.

Choice and non-choice tests were conducted. Trees were planted using a randomized block design. In the choice test, marked adult beetles were released at nine points diagonally distributed in the field. Trees were checked for presence of released beetles, adult feeding, egg sites and exit holes. In the no-choice test, a pair of adults (one male and one female) were caged with individual trees, which also were checked for adult feeding, oviposition sites and exit holes. Adult longevity was also recorded for all caged beetles.

As we expected, exit holes of adult beetles were found on *Acer mono*, *Acer platanoides*, *Acer saccharum*, and *Betula papyrifera*, *Salix matsudana*, *Ulmus pumila*, and several species of poplar (*Populus spp.*). However, unexpectedly, we also found exit holes on *Alnus incana*. Exit holes were also found on *Elaeagnus augustifolia*. No exit holes were found on some poplar species and hybrids such as *Populus deltoids*, *Populus alba* × *Populus glandulosa* and *Populus alba* × *Populus alba var. pyramidalis*. Although feeding and oviposition sites have been found on trees such as *Armeniaca sp.*, *Fraxinus chinensis*, *Fraxinus pennsylvanica*, *Malus pumila*, *Platanus occidentalis*, *Pyrus sp.*, *Quercus alba*, *Robinia pseudoacasia*, and *Sophora japonica*, no exit holes have been found on these trees. We observed that the number of egg pits made does not always agree with number of active egg sites and number of exit holes in both choice and non-choice test.

Two primary problems for this experiment were the different sizes of trees and presence of woodpeckers in the choice test plot. We did not know how tree size influenced oviposition and feeding. However, we know that the species planted were of different sizes (diameter and crown) because of different growth ratios and the different sizes initially planted.

VIBURNUM LEAF BEETLE: UPDATE ON A RECENTLY ARRIVED LANDSCAPE PEST

Paul A. Weston

Department of Entomology, Cornell University, 150 Insectary, Ithaca, NY 14853

Abstract

Viburnum leaf beetle, *Pyrrhalta viburni* (Paykull), is a European pest that was first detected in the U.S. in Maine in 1994. Since that time, it has spread through much of New England and New York, and is poised to invade much of the eastern half over the country over time. An additional, isolated invasion of the U.S. occurred in 2004 in Washington State, the result of spread from a separate population established in British Columbia, Canada. I present updated information on recent spread of the pest in New York and adjacent states, a revised list of species susceptibility to *P. viburni*, and results of laboratory testing of thermal requirements for egg hatch and immature development.

Eggs require a prolonged chilling period followed by warm temperatures for hatching; we have found the chilling period to be approximately 5 months at 5 °C. As expected, larval development was greatly accelerated with temperature between 17 and 22 °C, but then levelled off at 27 °C. Temperatures of 27 °C or higher are likely above the threshold for normal development because larval survival decreased and physical abnormalities were observed in resulting adults at this temperature.

Owing to the prolonged chilling requirement and abnormal larval development at 27 °C, it is likely that warm winter and spring temperatures will limit southern range expasion of *P. viburni* in the U.S. Availability of host material will not likely limit expansion because members of the arrowwood complex (one of the most suitable hosts for the pest) are distributed throughout nearly all of the eastern half of the country. Westward spread will likely be determined largely by distribution of native hosts, which become less common in the Great Plains.

APPLICATION OF REMOTE SENSING TECHNOLOGY TO EMERALD ASH BORER SURVEY

David Williams[1], David Bartels[2], Alan Sawyer[1] and Victor Mastro[1]

[1]USDA, APHIS, Pest Survey, Detection, and Exclusion Laboratory, Building 1398, Otis ANGB, MA 02542
[2]USDA, APHIS, Pest Detection, Diagnostic, and Management Laboratory, Moore Air Base, Building 6414, 22675 North Moorefield Road, Edinburg, TX 78541

Abstract

Conventional ground survey for emerald ash borer (EAB) is difficult and time-consuming. Detection of new infestations outside the quarantine area is often haphazard, relying on chance sighting and reporting by citizens. EAB ground survey is especially problematic because all stages but the adult are spent inside the host tree, where signs of their presence are not readily evident. Thus, the survey for new EAB infestations using remote sensing holds great appeal from the standpoints of both ease and economic efficiency. We initiated this project in the summer of 2003 with the primary goal to develop maps of ash trees at risk from EAB for use by federal and state survey personnel. We made significant progress during the 2004 season. Four basic activities were necessary to meet our objectives: image acquisition, collection of spectral signatures for ash trees and other tree species, collection of ground truth information on ash trees and other hardwood species recorded in the imagery, and image analysis and map development.

Our remote sensing approach was hyperspectral imagery (HSI). SpecTIR Inc. of California collected aerial HSI for us in 2004. Their HyperSpecTIR sensor simultaneously recorded reflectance from trees and other ground features over 227 spectral bands ranging from visible light through shortwave infrared wavelengths. Images were collected over three flight lines in southern Michigan and three in northwestern Ohio. Individual flight lines were 2 kilometers wide and 15-40 kilometers long at ground spatial resolutions of one and two meters. Images were collected twice during the 2004 season, in early July and late August. These times represented periods of relatively low and high stress, respectively, due to beetle activity and water availability.

During the data collection flights, we were joined by several collaborators, including scientists from ITT Aerospace Sciences, Clark University, and the USDA Forest Service. These collaborations were very productive, especially in getting HSI experts to the field to observe and discuss the technical details of the data collection.

One part of our activities on the ground was the collection of spectral signatures of ash trees and other tree species using a hand-held spectrometer. This work addresses two main questions: Can HSI distinguish ash trees from those of other hardwood species? Can it separate stressed ash trees from healthy ash trees? A fundamental goal of the spectrometry is to build spectral libraries of (1) different hardwood tree species at different stages of phenology over the growing season; and (2) ash trees over a range of EAB infestation and other ashes under stress by manual girdling and herbicide injections.

This work will assess the feasibility of distinguishing tree species using spectral characteristics. Preliminary work in 2003 using an ASD FieldSpec Pro spectrometer (which recorded spectral bands from the visible spectrum to shortwave infrared) indicated that tree species, including oak, walnut, maple, and cherry, were distinguishable from ash a high percentage of the time based on leaf signatures. Ash trees that had been girdled or treated with herbicide were also distinguishable from healthy ash at the leaf level. During the 2004 growing season, leaf level data were collected four times from June to September in replicated experimental plots set up by Michigan State University and USDA Forest Service to investigate signatures of stressed ash trees.

Around the time of the hyperspectral flights, large numbers of spectral signatures were collected from over 15 tree species under our flight lines in Michigan and Ohio. These data are being analyzed to help in classifying the airborne HSI. This work utilized the APHIS bucket truck so that measurements could be made above tree crowns, replicating the perspective of the airborne sensor.

Ground truth data were collected during five missions throughout 2004. Three hundred ash trees in various states of decline and over 400 trees of other species were identified under the flight lines. We were especially interested in species that are often confused with ash, such as boxelder, hickory, and walnut. Ground truth observations typically consisted of GPS locations of individual trees along with notes as to their size and condition and digital photos. Ground truth data will be used to develop models for mapping ash and to validate those models.

The data sets for each HSI flight totaled over 150 gigabytes. Because of their sheer size, we distributed them on large external hard drives. As of early November 2004, all data were in the hands of our collaborators, and the analysis is currently under way. Our collaborators bring many years of experience and considerable expertise to the analysis. As a result, we look forward to very productive results from our collective efforts in 2005.

LABORATORY EVALUATION OF SEMIOCHEMICAL DISPENSERS: A THEORETICAL CHEMICAL KINETIC APPROACH TO THE EMISSION RATE OF DISPARLURE ACTIVE INGREDIENT

Aijun Zhang

USDA, Agriculture Research Services, Chemicals Affecting Insect Behavior Laboratory Beltsville Agriculture Research Center-West, 10300 Baltimore Ave. Beltsville, MD 20705

Abstract

Emission rate of active ingredient is a critical factor to affect efficacy of semiochemical dispensers in pest management. From an insect pest management standpoint, it is desirable to have a device that could release the semiochemical at a constant rate. In practice, such a device may be difficult to realize. Capillaries as controlled-release devices have been developed since 1980. However, many of reports indicated that pheromone-charged fibers used commercially in insect control strategies performed in poor agreement with the predicted release rate (Weatherston et al. 1985a, Weatherston et al. 1985b). Currently, the most popular and economical semiochemicals release vehicles are still the classical controlled-release devices, such as plastic, rubber, laminate, microcapsules, rope, etc. Measuring vapor phase (absorbate analysis) and examining the residual content (weight loss or solvent extraction analysis) of the samples exposed in the laboratory or the field are the widely used methods to obtain the emission rate. However, the disadvantage of these classical methods is time consuming, requiring months or years to get the results (Warthen et al. 1998a, Warthen et al. 1998b). Sometimes the determination is difficult, e.g., determining emission rates at below room temperature.

In order to quickly obtain the emission rate at any temperature and save the time, a theoretical chemical kinetic approach has been deployed. It is hypothesized that volatile active ingredients are desorbed from absorbent type controlled-release devices following first order kinetics ($-dc/dt = kc$), which is proved to be valid for acetates and alcohols in polyethylene tubing (Bradley et al. 1995, McDonough et al. 1992) and rubber septa dispensers (McDonough 1991). This hypothesis was tested in this study using seven different disparlure formulations including three commercial disparlure formulations from Hercon Environmental Inc. (flakes and laminate tape), one from Trécé Inco. (string), three formulation from Shin-Etsu Chemical Co., Ltd., and one laboratory made red natural rubber septum formulation at six different temperatures (50, 55, 60, 65, 70, and 75 °C) in the oven for 4 days. The airflow through the system was maintained at 10 L/min by a valve on the hose vacuum source and the airspeed over the dispensers within the oven chamber was calculated to be 0.32 cm/sec. Three samples from each temperature were taken out every 24 h, extracted with certain amount of solvent for 48 h, and the amount of residual disparlure was determined by a capillary GC.

Experimentally it was found that first-order hypothesis was valid to all tested formulations. When the function percentage concentrations of disparlure determined at different temperature were plotted against the function time the exponential decay curves ($C/C_0 = e^{-kt}$) were displayed. After logarithm transformation ($\ln C/C_0 = -kt$), the straight lines were obtained with the linear regression coefficients, R^2, about 0.9. The rate constants (k) at each temperature and each formulation can be obtained from the slopes of each line.

An important property of a first-order kinetic is the half-life time ($t_{1/2}$). That is the time required for the concentration of disparlure to decrease to half its initial value. Half-life time ($t_{1/2}$) of first-order kinetics is independent on concentration. In all of other order kinetics, half-life time ($t_{1/2}$) is the function of concentration. So that the rate constant (k) of first-order kinetics can be obtained by an equation: $k = 0.693/t_{1/2}$, or half-life time ($t_{1/2}$) can be obtained by an equation: $t_{1/2} = k/0.693$.

The relation between the rate constant (k) and absolute temperature (T) was first proposed by Arrheniuis:

$$k = Ae^{-E/RT}$$

Where: A = *frequency factor*   R = *gas constant*
E = activation energy T = absolute temperature
Activation energy of each formulation can be obtained from equation, $\ln k = -E/RT + A$. If the function $\ln k$ for various temperatures is plotted against the function 1/T, the activation energy (E) is equal to the slope of the straight line times the gas constant R (Fig. 1). After determination of activation energy (E), the rate constant (k) at any temperature can be calculated by Arrheniuis equation: $\ln k_2/k_1 = E/R\,(T_2-T_1/T_2T_1)$, and the longevity of the formulation, half-life time ($t_{1/2}$), can be easily obtained (Fig. 2 and 3).

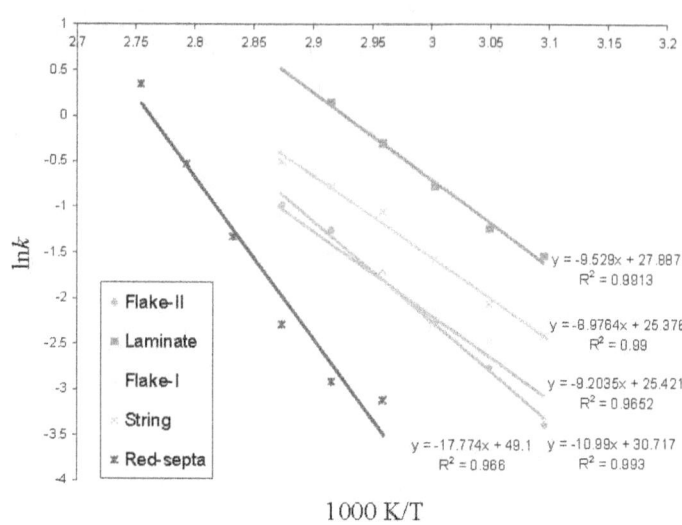

Figure 1.—Result of activation energy of disparlure dispensers (2003)

Overall, the apparent activation energies (E) and rate constants (k) of all tested dispensers have been determined based on experimental data, and therefore the longevities of the formulation, half-life time ($t_{1/2}$), at any different temperature can be calculated. The values of half-life time ($t_{1/2}$) of tested formulations are compatible to those obtained from green hose ageing study (Fig. 2 and 3). Therefore, these parameters can be used as standards to evaluate the dissemination of active ingredient from different semiochemical dispensers at different temperature conditions.

References

Bradley, S.J., Suckling, D.M., McNaughon, K.G., Wearing, C.H., and Karg, G. 1995. **A temperature-dependent model for predicting release rates of pheromone from a polyethylene tubing dispenser.** J. Chem. Ecol. 21: 745-760.

McDonough, L.M. 1991. **Controlled release of insect sex pheromones from a natural rubber substrate,** pp. 106-124, *In* P. Hedin (ed.). Naturally Occurring Pest Bioregulators. ACS Symposium Series No. 449. American Chemical Society, Washington D.C.

McDonough, L.M., Aller, W.C., and Knight, A.L. 1992. **Performance characteristics of commercial controlled-release dispenser of sex pheromone for control of codling moth (*Cydia pomonella*) by mating disruption.** J. Chem. Ecol. 18: 2177-2189.

Warthen, J.D., Cunningham, R.T., Leonhardt, B.A., Cook, J.M., Avery, J.W., and Harte, E.M. 1998a. **Comparison of ceralure and trimedlure controlled release formulations for male Mediterranean fruit flies in C&C traps.** J. Chem. Ecol. 24: 1305-1314.

Warthen, J.D., Mitchell, E.R., and Harte, E.M. 1998b. **Laboratory release rate studies of Shin-Etsu, freshly manufactured versus cold-stored, fresh pheromone ropes.** J. Environ. Sci. Health, Part A 33: 701-714.

Weatherston, I., Miller, D., and Dohse, L. 1985a. **Capillaries as controlled release devices for insect pheromones and other volatile substances—a reevaluation. Part I. Kinetics and development of predictive model for glass capillaries.** J. Chem. Ecol. 11: 953-966.

Weatherston, I., Miller, D., and Lavoie-Dornik, J. 1985b. **Capillaries as controlled release devices for insect pheromones and other volatile substances—a reevaluation. Part II. Predicting release rates from Celcon and Teflon capillaries.** J. Chem. Ecol. 11: 967-978.

Table 1.—Result of disparlure emission rate study (2003)

Dispenser	$t_{1/2}$ (day)			
	Kinetic			Green House
	15 °C	25 °C	35 °C	
Laminate (500 μg)	136	45	16	
String (500 μg)	244	86	32	
Flake (I) (200 μg)	398	136	50	67
Flake (II) (200 μg)	1,155	320	97	99
Red Septa (1000 μg)	210,000	23,650	3,777	
	(575Y)	(72Y)	(10Y)	

Table 2.—Result of disparlure emission rate study (2004)

Dispenser	Kinetic			Green House
	R^2	$t_{1/2}$*	R^2	$t_{1/2}$**
Flake (I) (172 μg)	0.9523	101	0.7051	102
Shin-Etsu A (123 μg)	0.9922	58	0.9772	80
Shin-Etsu C (76 μg)	0.9776	34	0.9753	62
Shin-Etsu NI (97 μg)	0.8634	39	0.8494	86

R^2= liner regression coefficient
*half-life time (day, 25 °C, calcul.)
** half-life time (day, 27 °C, obser.).

POSTER DISPLAYS 2005

Potential Use of Parasitic Wasps to Control New Exotic Wood-Boring Species of Insects on Trees of Economic Importance in Indiana. Arcinas, R., Sadof, C.

Double Electrode Voltage Clamping as a Technique to Assess Susceptibility to *Bt* Toxins, Borchardt, Deanna, D'Amico, V., Keil, C., Hock, G.

Arborjet Approach and Use of Stem Micro-Infusion Treatments ror the Management of Specific Insect Pests and Physiological Diseases in Forest, Landscape and Plantation Trees. Doccola, J. Wild, P., Bristol, E., Lojko, J.

The Douglas-fir Beetle in Minnesota: Locating an Indigenous Exotic in Northern Forests. Dodds, Kevin J., Gilmore, D., Seybold, S.J.

Getting the Word Out: FHTET and Invasive. org Collaborations. Douce, G., Reardon, R., Moorhead, D., Bargeron, C., Evans, C.

Don't Let Cacto Blast US! : A Cooperative Effort to Detect and Test Containment of the Cactus Moth, *Cactoblastis cactorum* on the US Gulf Coast. Floyd, J., Bloem, K., Bloem, S., Carpenter, J., Hight, S.

Effects of Age on Reproductive Response of *Glyptapanteles flavicoxis*, a Parasitoid of the Gypsy Moth. Fuester, R., Taylor, P., Swan, K., Ramaseshiah, G.

Cellulose Digestion in Larvae of the Asian Longhorned Beetle. Geib, S., Jones, D., Hoover, K.

A Highly Effective Tree Injection Method Using Imidacloprid for the Control Of Emerald Ash Borer. Helson, B., Thompson, D., McKenzie, N., Otis, G.

Testing Potential Natural Enemies of *Anoplophora glabripennis* and *A. Chinensis.* Hérard, F., Lopez, J., Cocquempot, C., Maspero, M.

Effects of Timing of Larval Chill on *Anoplophora glabripennis* (Coleoptera: Cerambycidae) Survival and Pupation. Keena, M.

Commercially Available Traps and Lures for Detecting Nun Moth, *Lymantria monacha* L., in North America. Lance, D., Schaeffer, P., Sawyer, A., Mastro, V., Gonschorrek, J., Kolb, M., Sukovata, L., Yurchenko, G.

Chlortetracycline Enhances Survival of Larval *Anoplophora glabripennis* Reared on Artificial Diet. Lance, D., Holske, B.,

Method for the Extraction and Analysis of Imidacloprid Residues in Plant Material by Enzyme-linked Immunosorbent Assay (ELISA). Lewis, P., Molongoski, J., Hagan, J.

New Pest Advisory Group Web-Accessible Database. McCullum, N.

The USDA APHIS PPQ New Pest Advisory Group (NPAG): Assessing New and Imminent Exotic Plant Pests in the United States. McCullum, N., Devorshak, C., Scott, S., Hilary, H.

Asian Longhorned Beetle Host Preferences Among 24 Landscape Tree Species. Morewood, D., Sellmer, J., Hoover, K.

Efficacy of Microwave Irradiation of Wood Pallet Materials for Eradication of Pinewood Nematode and Wood-boring Insects. Morewood, D., Kimmel, J., Hoover, K., Halbrendt, J., Janowiak, J.

Winter Mortality in *Adelges tsugae* Populations in 2003 And 2004. Shields, K., Cheah, C.

Restoration of the American Elm in Forested Landscapes. Slavicek, J., Balser, D., Boose, A., Cavender, N.

Production of LdNPV in Cell Culture Bioreactors. Slavicek, J., Gabler, M.

Does Community Structure Influence Forest Susceptibility and Response to Emerald Ash Borer?. Smith, Annemarie, Herms, D., Long, R.

The First Natural Enemies of Emerald Ash Borer Found in China. Strazanac, John S., Yang, Z.

Weed-US: A Database of Plants Invading Natural Areas in the United States. Swearingen, J.

Beauveria bassiana for Control of the Brown Spruce Longhorn Beetle, *Tetropium fuscum* (fabr.) (Coleoptera: Cerambycidae). Sweeney, J., Thurston, G., Lavallée, R., Trudel, R., Desrochers, P., Côté, C., Guertin, C., Todorova, S., Kope, H H., Alfaro, R.

Parasitism of the Brown Spruce Longhorn Beetle, *Tetropium fuscum* (Fabr.) (Coleoptera: Cerambycidae) in Halifax, Nova Scotia. Sweeney, J., Price, J., Sopow, S., Smith, G., Broad, G., Goulet, Henri, Bennett, A.

Investigating the Role of the Cadherin-like Protein from *Lymantria dispar* as a *Bacillus thuringiensis* Cry1A Toxin Receptor. Valaitis, A., Garner, K., Jurat-Fuentes, J., Adang, M.

A Novel Elastase-like Protein from *Lymantria dispar* is Involved in the Proteolytic Activation of *Bacillus thuringiensis* Cry1A Protoxins in *Lymantria dispar*. Valaitis, A.

Viburnum Leaf Beetle: Update on a Recently Arrived Landscape Pest. Weston, P., Desurmont, G.

Host Plant Preferences of the Periodical Cicada, *Magicicada septendecim*. Zuefle, M., Tallamy, D., D'Amico, V.

Assessing New Strains of LdNPV for Use in Gypchek: NL-203 and WT-203. D'Amico, V., Slavicek, J., Podgwaite, J.

Preliminary Assessment of the Cold Tolerance of *Laricobius nigrinus*, a Winter Active Predator of the Hemlock Woolly Adelgid. Humble, L. Mavin, L.

Forest Protection Maps of Siberia and the Russian Far East. Baranchikov, Y., McFadden, M., Korets, M.

Host Specificity of Gypsy Moth Microsporidia: Field Studies in Slovakia. Solter, L., Pilarska, D., McManus, M., Novotny, J., Zubrik, M., Patocka, J.

Regional Pest Risk Assessments for Invasive Species. Venette, R.

Quantifying Transmission of Microsporidia in the Field. Hoch, G., D'Amico, V., Solter, L., McManus, M., Zubrik, M.

The Role of Tree-fall Gaps in the Invasion of Exotic Plants in Forests: the Case of *Rubus phoenicolasius Maxim* (Rosaceae) in Maryland, USA. Gorchov, D.L., Whigham, D.F., Innis, A.F., Miles, B., O'Neill, J.

Emerald Ash Borer (*Agrilus planipennis*) Studies on Adult Collection and Trapping Methods. Fraser, I., Francese, J.A., Lance, D.R., Mastro, V.C., Oliver, J.B., Weed, A., Youssef, N.

MISSING PRESENTATION ABSTRACTS FROM THE 2005 USDA RESEARCH FORUM

The Nature Conservancy's efforts to address invasive species: What role for the scientific community? Frank Lowenstein

Incorporating population ecology science to improve strategies for managing biological invasions. Andrew Liebhold

Invasive patterns of *Cameraria ohridella* in Germany, France, and United Kingdom: the effect of long-distance dispersal and human population density. Marius Gilbert

Allee effects in invasive species: the discrepancy between models and data. John Drake

Arrival rate of non-indigenous insect species into the United States through foreign trade. Deborah McCullough

Winter moth: a new invasive species in New England. Joe Elkinton

Recent progress in research on Japanese oak wilt. Naoto Kamata

Geographical variation in the synchrony and periodicity of gypsy moth outbreaks. Derek Johnson

The Asian gypsy moth monitoring program in Russia and Japan. Steve Munson

***Phytophthora ramorum:* Current status.** James Writer

Emerald ash borer in North America: current status and U.S. program response. Craig Kellogg

Toward the development of survey trapping methodology for EAB. Therese Poland

Controlling emerald ash borer with insecticides. Deborah McCullough

Asian longhorned beetle program in the United States. Christine Markham

Asian longhorned beetle in Greater Toronto: program overview. Ben Gasman

Dispersal of adult ALB and its implications for program management. Alan Sawyer

Potential Use of Parasitic Wasps to Control New Exotic Wood-Boring Species of Insects on Trees of Economic Importance in Indiana. R. Arcinas and C. Sadof

Forest Protection Maps of Siberia and the Russian Far East. Y. Baranchikov, M. McFadden, and M. Korets

Double Electrode Voltage Clamping as a Technique to Assess Susceptibility to *Bt* Toxins. Deanna Borchardt, V. D'Amico, C. Keil, and G. Hock

Assessing New Strains of LdNPV for Use in Gypchek: NL-203 and WT-203. V. D'Amico, J. Slavicek, and J. Podgwaite

The Douglas-fir Beetle in Minnesota: Locating an Indigenous Exotic in Northern Forests. Kevin Dodds, D. Gilmore, and S.J. Seybold

Emerald Ash Borer (*Agrilus planipennis*) studies on adult collection and trapping methods. I. Fraser, J.A. Francese, D.R. Lance, V.C. Mastro, J.B. Oliver, A. Weed, and N. Youssef

New Pest Advisory Group Web-Accessible Database. N. McCullum

The USDA APHIS PPQ New Pest Advisory Group (NPAG): Assessing New and Imminent Exotic Plant Pests in the United States. N. McCullum, C. Devorshak, S. Scott, and H. Hilary

Asian longhorned beetle host preferences among 24 landscape tree species. D. Morewood, J. Sellmer, and K. Hoover

Efficacy of microwave irradiation of wood pallet materials for eradication of pinewood nematode and wood-boring insects. D. Morewood, J. Kimmel, K. Hoover, J. Halbrendt, and J. Janowiak

Regional pest risk assessments for invasive species. R. Venette

Host plant preferences of the periodical cicada, *Magicicada septendecim,*. M. Zuefle, D. Tallamy, and V. D'Amico

ATTENDEES

Robert Acciavatti
USDA Forest Service, FHP
180 Canfield Street
Morgantown, WV 26505
racciavatti@fs.fed.us

Kim Adams
SUNY-CESF, 125 Illick Hall
1 Forestry Drive
Syracuse, NY 13210
kbadams@syr.edu

Preston Aldrich
Benedictine University, Biology
5700 College Road
Lisle, IL 60532
paldrich@ben.edu

Douglas Allen
SUNY-CESF
1 Forestry Drive
Syracuse, NY 13210
dcallen@esf.edu

Rich Anacker
Maryland Dept. Agriculture
50 Harry S. Truman Pkwy.
Annapolis, MD 21401
anackerRH@mda.state.md.us

Judith Antipin
USDA Forest Service, FHP
11 Campus Blvd.
Newtown Square, PA 19073
jantipin@fs.fed.us

Allan Auclair
USDA APHIS, PPQ
4700 River Road
Riverdale, MD 20737
allan.auclair@aphis.usda.gov

John Baggett
Fairfax County FPM Section
12055 Government Center Pkwy.
Fairfax, VA 22035
John.Baggett@fairfaxcounty.gov

John Bain
Forest Research, New Zealand
Private Bag 3020
Rotorua, New Zealand
john.bain@forestresearch.co.nz

Yuri Baranchikov
VN Sukachev Institute of Forest
Akademgorodok
Krasnoyarsk, 660036, Russia
Baranchikov_Yuri@yahoo.com

David Bartels
USDA APHIS, PPQ
22675 NN. Moorefield Rd., #6414
Edinburg, TX 78541
David.W.Bartels@aphis.usda.gov

Dick Bean
Maryland Dept. Agriculture
50 Harry S. Truman Pkwy.
Annapolis, MD 21401
beanra@mda.state.md.us

Philip Bell
USDA, APHIS, PPQ
920 Main Campus Dr., Ste. 200
Raleigh, NC 27606
philip.d.bell@aphis.usda.gov

Robert Bennett
USDA-ARS, BARC-E, Bldg. 306
10300 Baltimore Ave.
Beltsville, MD 20705
bennettr@ba.ars.usda.gov

E. Michael Blumenthal
PA Bureau of Forestry, DCNR
208 Airport Drive
Middletown, PA 17057
eblumentha@state.pa.us

Michael Bohne
USDA Forest Service
320 Merrick Road
Amityville, NY 11701
mbohne@fs.fed.us

DeAnna Borchardt
University of Delaware
246 Townsend Hall
Newark, DE 19717
borchard@udel.edu

J. Robert Bridges
USDA Forest Service
11 Campus Blvd., Ste. 200
Newtown Square, PA 19073
rbridges@fs.fed.us

Susan A. Bright
USDA, APHIS, PPQ
4700 River Road, Unit 150
Riverdale, MD 20737
susan.a.bright@aphis.usda.gov

Eric Bristol
Arborjet, Inc.
70B Cross Street
Winchester, MA 01890
ericbristol.fed.us

Bill Brown
University of Delaware
253A Townsend Hall
Newark, DE 19717
wpbrown@udel.edu

Paul Brown
JJ Mauget Co.
5435 Peck Road
Arcadia, CA 91006
paul@mauget.com

Rose Buckner
Maryland Dept. Agriculture
50 Harry S. Truman Pkwy.
Annapolis, MD 21401
bucknerm@mda.state.md.us

Stephen Bullington
USDA APHIS, PPQ
401 E.Louther St., Ste. 102
Carlisle, PA 17013
Stephen.W.Bullington@aphis.usda.gov

Charlie Burnham
Massachusetts Dept. of Conservation
P.O. Box 484
Amherst, MA 01004
Charlie.Burnham@state.ma.us

Helen Butalla
USDA Forest Service
180 Canfield Street
Morgantown, WV 26505
hbutalla@fs.fed.us

Faith Campbell
The Nature Conservancy
4245 North Fairfax Drive
Arlington, VA 22203
fcampbell@tnc.org

Nicole Campbell
USDA APHIS, PPQ
900 Northrop Road, Ste. C
Wallingford, CT 06492
Nicole.K.Campbell@aphis.usda.gov

Ross Campbell
US GAP
441 G Street, NW
Washington, DC 20548
campbellr@gao.gov

Sally Cannon
Maryland Dept. Agriculture
P.O. Box 178
Cheltenham, MD 20623
southernfpm@erols.com

Dave Cohen
Maryland Dept. Agriculture
3 Pershing Street, Rm. 100
Cumberland, MD 21502
mdafpm@hereintown.net

Jason Cole
Helicopter Applicators, Inc.
1670 York Rd.
Gettysburg, PA 17325
jcole@helicopterapplicators.com

Karen Coluzzi
Maine Dept. Agriculture
28 State House Station
Augusta, ME 04333
Karen.I.Coluzzi@maine.gov

Joseph Cook
USDA Forest Service
180 Canfield St.
Morgantown, WV 26505
jlcook@fs.fed.us

Thomas Corell
Earth BioSciences, Inc.
106 Somerset Avenue
Fairfield, CT 06824
thomascorrell@sbcglobal.net

Richard Cowles
CT Agricultural Expt. Stn.
123 Huntington Street
New Haven, CT 06504
Richard.Cowles@po.state.us

Don Dagnan
USDA Forest Service
11 Campus Blvd.
Newtown Square, PA 19073
dcdagnan@fs.fed.us

Vince D'Amico, III
USDA Forest Service
c/o University of Delaware
Newark, DE 19717
vdamico@elbowfarm.com

John Davis
USDA ARS, Bldg. 007, Rm. 301
10300 Baltimore Ave.
Beltsville, MD 20705
davisj@ba.ars.usda.gov

Peter deGroot
Canadian Forest Service
1219 Queen Street
Sault Ste. Marie, Ontario
pdegroot@nrcan.gc.ca

Don Diamond
JJ Mauget Co.
5435 Peck Road
Arcadia, CA 91006
dondiamond@aol.com

Joseph Dickens
USDA ARS, Bldg. 007, Rm. 301
10300 Baltimore Ave.
Beltsville, MD 20705
dickensj@ba.ars.usda.gov

Andrea Diss
Wisconsin Dept. Nat. Resources
P.O. Box 7921
Madison, WI 53707
dissa@dnr.state.wi.us

Joseph Doccola
Arborjet, Inc.
70B Cross Street
Winchester, MA 01890
joedoccola@arborjet.com

John Dodd
USDA APHIS
4700 River Road
Riverdale, MD 20737
john.t.dodd@aphis.usda.gov

Kevin Dodds
USDA Forest Service
271 Mast Road
Durham, NH 03824
kdodds@fs.fed.us

Nathan Dodds
JJ Mauget Co.
5435 Peck Road
Arcadia, CA 91006
nate@mauget.com

G. Keith Douce
University of Georgia
P.O. Box 748
Tifton, GA 31793
kdouce@arches.uga.edu

Alan Dowdy
USDA APHIS, PPQ
1730 Varsity Drive, Ste. 400
Raleigh, NC 27606
alan.k.dowdy@aphis.usda.gov

John Drake
Nat. Ctr. Ecological Analysis &
Synthesis
735 State Street, Ste. 300
Santa Barbara, CA 93101-3351
drake@nceas.ucsb.edu

Tom Dudley
University of Nevada
MS 186, 1000 Valley Road
Reno, NV 89512-0013
tdudley@cabnr.unr.edu

Adrian Duehl
North Carolina State University
Entomology, Box 7626
Raleigh, NC 27695
Adrian.Duehl@ncsu.edu

Don Duerr
USDA Forest Service
1720 Peachtree Rd. NW
Atlanta, GA 30309
dduerr@fs.fed.us

Donald Eggen
PA Bureau of Forestry, DCNR
208 Airport Drive, 2nd Floor
Middletown, PA 17057-5027
deggen@state.pa.us

Joseph Elkinton
University of Massachusetts
Fernald Hall
Amherst, MA 01003
Elkinton@ent.umass.edu

Jodie Ellis
Purdue University, Smith Hall
901 W. State Street
West Lafayette, IN 47907
ellisj@purdue.edu

Roeland Elliston
USDA APHIS, PPQ
2150 Centre Avenue
Ft. Collins, CO 80526
roeland.j.Elliston@aphis.usda.gov

Thomas Elliott
USDA Forest Service
180 Canfield Street
Morgantown, WV 26505
telliott@fs.fed.us

Barry Emens
USDA, APHIS, PPQ
P.O. Box 330
Trenton, NJ 08625
barry.c.emens@aphis.usda.gov

Michelle Every
Maryland Dept. Agriculture
50 Harry S. Truman Pkwy.
Annapolis, MD 21401
everymk@state.md.us

Mary Ann Fajvan
USDA Forest Service
180 Canfield Street
Morgantown, WV 26505
mfajvan@fs.fed.us

Claudia Ferguson
USDA APHIS, PPQ
201 Varick Street
New York, NY 10014
Claudia.Ferguson@usda.gov

Frank Finch
Fairfax County FPM Section
12055 Government Center Pkwy.
Fairfax, VA 22035
frank.finch@fairfaxcounty.gov

Richard Fine
USDA APHIS, PPQ
325 Mercer Corp. Blvd.
Robbinsville, NJ 08690
richard.r.fine@aphis.usda.gov

Joel Floyd
USDA APHIS, PPQ
4700 River Road, Unit 137
Riverdale, MD 20737
joel.floyd@aphis.usda.gov

Gerald Fowler
M7 Visual Intelligence
116 Industrial Park Crescent
Sault Ste, Marie, ONT CA P6B 5P2
intnl@sympatico.ca

Ivich Fraser
USDA, APHIS, PPQ
5936 Ford Ct.
Brighton, MI 48116
ivich.fraser@aphis.usda.gov

N. Mark Frick
M7 Visual Intelligence
510 Bering Drive, Ste. 310
Houston, TX 77057
mark@visidata.com

Roger W. Fuester
USDA-ARS, BIIRL
501 S. Chapel Street
Newark, DE 19713
roger.fuester@udel.edu

Weyman Fussell
USDA APHIS, PPQ
4700 Rive Road
Riverdale, MD 20737
weyman.fussell@aphis.usda.gov

Jeff Gallagher
Prince William County
4092 Merchant Plaza, Ste. A
Woodbridge, VA 22192
jgallagher@pwcgov.org

Ben Gasman
Canadian Food Inspection Agency
1124 Finch Ave. W, Unit #2
Downsview, Ontario M3J 2E2
gasmanb@inspection.gc.ca

Scott Geib
Pennsylvania State University
521 ASI Bldg., Entomology
University Park, PA 16802
smg283@psu.edu

Marius Gilbert
CP 160/12 Univ. Libre de Bruxelles
CV50 av. F.D. Roosevelt
B1050 Brussels, Belgium
mgilbert@ulb.ac.be

Nancy Gillette
USDA Forest Service
P.O. Box 245
Berkeley, CA 94701
ngillette@fs.fed.us

Joseph Gittleman
USDA APHIS, PPQ
320-01 Merrick Rd.
Amityville, NY 11701
joe.p.gittleman@aphis.usda.gov

David Gorchov
Miami University/Smithsonian Inst.
SERC, P.O. Box 28
Edgewater, MD 21037
gorchovdl@muohio.edu

Juli Gould
USDA APHIS, PPQ
Bldg. 1398
Otis ANGB, MA 02542
juil.r.gould@aphis.usda.gov

David Gray
Canadian Forest Service
P.O. Box 4000
Fredericton, NB, Canada E3B 5P7
dgray@nrcan.gc.ca

Sarah Green
Helicopter Applicators, Inc.
1670 York Road
Gettysburg, PA 17325
sgreen@helicopterapplicators.com

Gary Greer
Grand Valley State University
1 Campus Drive
Allendale, MI 49401
greerg@gvsu.edu

Nina Grimaldi
Maryland Dept. Agriculture
50 Harry S. Truman Pkwy.
Annapolis, MD 21401
grimalnc@mda.state.md.us

Kevin Hackett
USDA ARS, National Program Staff
5601 Sunnyside Avenue
Beltsville, MD 20705
kjh@ars.usda.gov

Fred Hain
North Carolina State University
Box 7626, Grinnells Lab.
Raleigh, NC 27695
fred_hain@ncsu.edu

Ann Hajek
Department of Entomology
Cornell University
Ithaca, NY 14853
aeh4@cornell.edu

Dennis Haugen
USDA Forest Service
1992 Folwell Avenue
St. Paul, MN 55108
dhaugen@fs.fed.us

Deborah Hayes
Maryland Dept. Agriculture
411 Franklin St.
Denton, MD 21629
fpmes@dmv.com

Jim Heath
Maryland Dept. Agriculture
27722 Nanticoke Rd., Unit 2
Salisbury, MD 21801
jheathg@goeaston.net

Dennis Heltzel
USDA APHIS, PPQ
5162 Valleypointe Pkwy. Rm. 101
Roanoke, VA 24019
dheltzel@aphis.usda.gov

Gordon Henry
Canadian Food Inspection Agency
59 Camelot Drive
Ottawa, Ontario K1A 0Y9
henryg@inspection.gc.ca

Franck Herard
USDA ARS, EBCL
Campus Internationale de Baillarguet
CS90013 Montferrier-sur-Lez, 34988
Saint-Gely-du-Fesc Cedex, France
fherard@ars-ebcl.org

Daniel Herms
Ohio State University/OARDC
1680 Madison Ave.
Wooster, OH 44691
herms.2@osu.edu

Robert Heyd
Michigan Dept. Natural Resources
1990 US 41 South
Marquette, MI 49855
Heydr@michigan.gov

Shelley Hicks
Maryland Department of Agriculture
50 Harry S. Truman Pkwy.
Annapolis, MD 21401
mdagreenhouse@erols.com

Gernot Hoch
BOKU - Univ. of Natural Resources
Hasenauerstrasse 38
A-1190 Vienna, Austria
hoch@ento.boku.ac.at

E. Richard Hoebeke
Dept. Entomology, Comstock Hall
Cornell University
Ithaca, NY 14853
erh2@cornell.edu

Carol Holko
Maryland Department of Agriculture
50 Harry S. Truman Pkwy.
Annapolis, MD 21401
HolkoCA@mda.state.md.us

Kelli Hoover
Pennsylvania State University
Department of Entomology
State College, PA 16801
kxh25@psu.edu

Anthony Hopkin
Canadian Forest Service
1219 Queen St. E
Sault Ste. Marie, Ontario P6A 2E5
ahopkin@nrcan.gc.ca

Tracy Horner
USDA APHIS, PPD
4700 River Road
Riverdale, MD 20737
Tracy.A.Horner@aphis.usda.aphis

Cynthia Huebner
USDA Forest Service
180 Canfield Street
Morgantown, WV 26505
chuebner@fs.fed.us

Leland Humble
Canadian Forest Service, NRC
506 W. Burnside Road
Victoria, British Columbia V8Z 1M5
lhumble@pfc.forestry.ca

Derek Johnson
Pennsylvania State University
501 ASI Bldg., Dept. Entomology
University Park, PA 16802
dmj10@psu.edu

Kathleen JR Johnson
Oregon Dept. Agriculture
635 Capitol St., NE
Salem, OR 97301
kjohnson@oda.state.or.us

Naoto Kamata
Kanazawa University
Kakuma, Kanazawa, Ishikawa
920-1192 Japan
kamatan@kenroku.kanazawa-u.ac.jp

Kim Kattouw
Ontario Ministry of Natural Resour.
70 Foster Drive
Sault Ste., Marie, ONT P6A 6V5
kim.kattouw@mnr.gov.on.ca

Melody Keena
USDA Forest Service
51 Mill Pond Rd.
Hamden, CT 06514
mkeena@fs.fed.us

Craig Kellogg
USDA APHIS, PPQ
5936 Ford Ct., Ste. 200
Brighton, MI 48116
craig.kellogg@aphis.usda.gov

Mark Kenis
CABI Bioscience Switzerland Ctr.
1 Rue des Griffons
2800 Delemont, Switzerland
m.kenis@cabi.org

Troy Kimoto
Canadian Food Inspection Agency
4321 Still Creek Dr., Fl. 4, Rm. 400
Burnaby. British Columbia V5C 6S7
kimotot@inspection.gc.ca

Carolyn Klass
Dept. Entomology, 4140 Comstock
Ithaca, NY 14853-2601
ck20@cornell.edu

Suzanne Klick
University of Maryland
11975 Homewood Road
Ellicott City, MD 21042
sklick@umd.edu

Daniel Kluza
US Environmental Protection Agency
1200 Pennsylvania Ave.
Washington, DC 20460
kluza.daniel@epamail.epa.gov

Kerrie Kyde
Maryland Dept. Natural Resources
580 Taylor Avenue
Annapolis, MD 21401
kkyde@dnr@state.md.us

James LaBonte
Oregon Dept. Agriculture
635 Capitol St., NE
Salem, OR 97301
jlabonte@oda.state.or.us

David Lance
USDA, APHIS, PPQ
Bldg. 1398
Otis ANGB, MA 02542
david.r.lance@aphis.usda.gov

Deborah Landau
The Nature Conservancy
5410 Grosvenor Lane, Ste. 100
Bethesda, MD 20850
dlandau@tnc.org

Charles Layton
Fairfax County Forest Pest Prg.
12055 Government Center Pkwy.
Fairfax, VA 22035
charles.Layton@fairfaxcounty.gov

Katharine Layton
Fairfax County Forest Pest Prg.
12055 Government Center Pkwy.
Fairfax, VA 22035
Katharine.layton@fairfaxcounty.gov

Donna Leonard
USDA Forest Service, FHP
200 WT Weaver Blvd.
Asheville, NC 28802
dleonard@fs.fed.us

Phil Lewis
USDA APHIS, PPQ
Bldg. 1398
Otis ANGB, MA 02542
philip.a.lewis@aphis.usda.gov

Andrew Liebhold
USDA Forest Service
180 Canfield Street
Morgantown, WV 26505
aliebhold@fs.fed.us

Harri Liljalehto
Ontario Ministry of Natural Resources
70 Foster Drive
Sault Ste. Marie, ONT P6A 6V5
c/o taylor.scarr@mnr.gov.on.ca

Frank Lowenstein
The Nature Conservancy
P.O. Box 268
Sheffield, MA 01257
flowenstein@tnc.org

Jacqueline Lu
NYC Parks & Recreation
24 W. 61st Street
New York, NY 10023
Jacqueline.lu@parks.nyc.gov

Jennifer Lund
Cornell University
19893 A Deckleman Rd.
Harrisburg, AR 72432
jlund96@yahoo.com

Tom Lupp
Maryland Dept. Agriculture
5305 F Spectrum Drive
Frederick, MD 21703
mdacent@erols.com

Barry Lyons
Canadian Forest Service
1219 Queen Street E
Sault Ste. Marie, Ontario P6A 2E5
blyons@nrcan.gc.ca

Bonnie MacCulloch
Vermont Agency of Agriculture
103 South Main Street
Waterbury, VT 05676
bmac@agr.state.vt.us

Martin MacKenzie
USDA Forest Service
180 Canfield Street
Morgantown, WV 26505
mmackenzie@fs.fed.us

Priscilla MacLean
Hercon Environmental
P.O. Box 435
Emigsville, PA 17318
pmaclean@herconenviorn.com

Stephen Malan
Maryland Dept. Agriculture
50 Harry S. Truman Pkwy.
Annapolis, MD 21401
malansc.mda.state.md.us

Mary Kay Malinoski
Maryland Coop. Ext. Svc.
12005 Homewood Road
Ellicott City, MD 21042
mkmal@umd.edu

C. Frederick Mann
USDA APHIS, PPQ, Rm. 350
50 Harry S. Truman Pkwy.
Annapolis, MD 21401
c.frederic.mann@aphis.usda.gov

Christine Markham
USDA APHIS, PPQ
920 Main Campus Dr., Ste. 200
Raleigh, NC 27606
christine.markham@aphis.usda.gov

James Marra
WA State Dept. Agriculture
3939 Cleveland Ave. SW
Olympia, WA 98501
jmarra@agr.wa.gov

Michael Marsh
West Virginia University
P.O. Box 6125
Morgantown, WV 26506-6125
mmarsh3@mix.wvu.edu

Philip Marshall
Indiana Division of Forestry
2782 W. County Rd. 540 S
Vallonia, IN 47281
pmarshall@hsonline.net

Debra Martin
Virginia Dept. Agric. & Cons. Aff.
1100 Bank Street, Washington Bldg.
Richmond, VA 23219
Debra.Martin@vdacs.Virginia.gov

Victor C. Mastro
USDA, APHIS, PPQ
Bldg. 1398
Otis ANGB, MA 02542
vic.mastro@aphis.usda.gov

Deborah McCullough
243 Natural Sciences Bldg.
Michigan State University
East Lansing, MI 48824
mccullod@msue.msu.edu

Nakieta McCullum
USDA APHIS, PPQ
1730 Varsity Dr., Ste. 300
Raleigh, NC 27606
nakieta.m.mccullum@aphis.usda.gov

Max W. McFadden
The Heron Group, LLC
P.O. Box 741
Georgetown, DE 19947
mcfadden@dca.net

Michael McManus
USDA Forest Service
51 Mill Pond Road
Hamden, CT 06514
mlmcmanus@fs.fed.us

Joe Meating
BioForest Technologies, Inc.
105 Bruce Street
Sault Ste. Marie, ONT P6A 2X6
jmeating@bioforest.ca

Bruce Miller
The Heron Group, LLC
P.O. Box 406
North East, PA 16428
bjmiller@psu.edu

Randall Morin
USDA-Forest Service
11 Campus Blvd., Ste. 200
Newtown Square, PA 19073
rsmorin@fs.fed.us

Steve Munson
USDA Forest Service
4746 S. 1900 E.
Ogden, UT 84403
smunson@fs.fed.us

Ellen Nibali
MD Ext. Home & Garden Info. Ctr.
12005 Homewood Road
Ellicott City, MD 21042
knibali@erols.com

Stephen Nicholson
Valent Biosciences Corporation
2704 Orser Rd.
Elginburg, Ontario K0H 1M0
stephen.nicholson@valent.com

Charlotte Nielsen
Cornell University
Dept. Entomology, Comstock Hall
Ithaca, NY 14853
cn49@cornell.edu

Rebecca Nisley
USDA Forest Service
51 Mill Pond Road
Hamden, CT 06514
rnisley@fs.fed.us

Larry Norton
Bayer Environmental Science
739 Blair Road
Bethlehem, PA 18017
larry.norton@bayercropscience.com

Robert Nowierski
USDA CSREES
800 9th Street
Washington, DC
rnowierski@

William Oldland
USDA Forest Service
180 Canfield Street
Morgantonw, WV 26505
woldland@fs.fed.us

James Oliver
USDA ARS, Bldg. 007, Rm. 301
10300 Baltimore Avenue
Beltsville, MD 20705
oliverj@ba.ars.usda.gov

Therese Poland
USDA Forest Service
1407 S. Harrison Road
East Lansing, MI 48823
tpoland@fs.fed.us

John Podgwaite
USDA Forest Service
51 Mill Pond Road
Hamden, CT 06514
jpodgwaite@fs.fed.us

Evan Preisser
University of Massachusetts
250 Natural Resources Rd.
Amherst, MA 01003
preisser@psis.umass.edu

Derek Puckett
USDA Forest Service
200 WT Weaver Blvd.
Asheville, NC 28804
dpuckett@fs.fed.us

P.C.Quimby
USDA ARS
Office of International Research Prg.
Beltsville, MD 20705
pcq@ars.usda.gov

Robert Rabaglia
Maryland Dept. Agriculture
50 Harry S. Truman Pkwy.
Annapolis, MD 21401
rabaglrj@mda.state.md.us

Iral Ragenovich
USDA Forest Service
P.O. Box 3623
Portland, OR 97208
iragenovich@fs.fed.us

Caroline Raisler
The Nature Conservancy
5410 Grosvenor Lane
Bethesda, MD 20814
craisler@tnc.org

Richard Reardon
USDA Forest Service, FHTET
180 Canfield Street
Morgantown, WV 26505
rreardon@fs.fed.us

Joanne Rebbeck
USDA Forest Service
359 Main Road
Delaware, OH 43105
jrebbeck@fs.fed.us

Kim Rice
Maryland Dept. Agriculture
50 Harry S. Truman Pkwy.
Annapolis, MD 21401
riceka@mda.state.md.us

Carlos Rodriguez
USDA ARS
5601 Sunnyside Ave.
Beltsville, MD 20705
carlos.Rodriguez@nps.ars.usda.gov

Alain Roques
INRA
Zoologie Forestière
BP 20619
F-45166 Olivet, France
Alain.roques@orleans.inra.fr

Mark Rothschild
Maryland Dept. Agriculture
27722 Nanticoke Rd., Unit 2
Salisbury, MD 21801
mjroths@attglobal.net

Vicente Sánchez
USDA Forest Service
51 Mill Pond Road
Hamden, CT 06514
vsanchez@fs.fed.us

Frank Sapio
USDA Forest Service
2150 Centre Ave., Bld. A, Ste. 331
Ft. Collins, CO 80526
fsapio@fs.fed.us

Al Sawyer
USDA, APHIS, PPQ
Bldg. 1398
Otis ANGB, MA 02542
alan.j.sawyer@aphis.usda.gov

Taylor Scarr
Ministry of Natural Resources
70 Foster Drive, Ste. 400
Sault Ste. Marie, Ontario P6A 6V5
taylor.scarr@mnr.gov.on.ca

Stephen Schmidt
NC Dept. Agriculture
1060 Mail Service Center
Raleigh, NC 27699-1060
stephen.Schmidt@ncmail.net

Paul Schaefer
USDA, ARS, BIIRL
501 S. Chapel St.
Newark, DE 19713
paulschaefer60@hotmail.com

Noel Schneeberger
USDA Forest Service
11 Campus Blvd., Ste. 200
Newtown Square, PA 19073
nschneeberger@fs.fed.us

Stacy Scott
USDA APHIS, PPQ
1017 Main Campus Dr., Ste. 1550
Raleigh, NC 27606
stacy.e.scott@usda.gov

Patricia Sellers
USDA Forest Service
401 Oakwood Drive
Harrisonburg, VA 220801
psellers@fs.fed.us

Gwen Servies
USDA APHIS PPQ
3920 North Rockwell
Chicago, IL 60618
gwen.servies@aphis.usda.gov

Troy Shaw
Fairfax County FPM Section
12055 Government Center Pkwy.
Fairfax, VA 22035
troy.shaw@fairfaxcounty.gov

Megan Sheremata
NY State Dept. Environ. Conserv.
47-40 21st St., 2nd Floor
Long Island City, NY 11101
mxsheremata@gw.dec.state.ny.us

Branislav Simic
NY State Dept. Agriculture & Markets
67-25 Dartmouth St.
Forest Hills, NY 11375
bransilav.simic@agmkt.state.ny.us

James Slavicek
USDA, Forest Service
359 Main Road
Delaware, OH 43015
jslavicek@fs.fed.us

Annemarie Smith
The Ohio State University
318 W. 12th St., 400 Aronoff Lab.
Columbus, OH 43210
smith.3746@osu.edu

John Smith
Bayer Environmental Science
4478 W. Woodpecker Lane
Trafalgar, IN 46181
john_f.smith@bayercropscience.com

Michael Smith
USDA ARS, BIIRL
501 S. Chapel Street
Newark, DE 19713
mtsmith@udel.edu

John Snitzer
Hood College
P.O.Box 38
Dickerson, MD 20842
navajuela@earthlink.net

Lee Solter
Illinois Natural History Survey
1101 W. Peabody Dr.
Urbana, IL 61801
lsolter@uiuc.edu

Sven-Erik Spichiger
PA Bureau of Forestry, DCNR
208 Airport Drive, 2nd Floor
Middletown, PA 17057-5027
sspichiger@state.pa.us

John Stanovick
USDA Forest Service
11 Campus Blvd., Ste. 200
Newtown Square, PA 19073
jstanovick@fs.fed.us

Mike Stefan
USDA APHIS, PPQ
4700 River Road
Riverdale, MD 20737
michael.b.stefan@usda.gov

Bruce Steward
Bayer Advanced
14930 Outlook Lane
Overland Park, KS 66223
bruce.steward@bayercropscience.com

James Stimmel
Bureau of Plant Industries
2301 N. Cameron Street
Harrisburg, PA 17110
jstimmel@state.pa.us

John Strazanac
West Virginia University
Ag. Sci. Bldg., Evansdale Dr.
Morgantown, WV 26506
jstrazanac@wvu.edu

Muriel Suffert
European Plant Protection
Organization
1 rue Le Nôtre
75016 Paris, France
hg@eppo.fr

Lidia Sukovata
Forest Research Institute
3, Bitwy Warszawskiej 1920
00-973 Warsaw, Poland
l.sukovata@ibles.waw.pl

Brian Sullivan
USDA Forest Service
2500 Shreveport Highway
Pineville, LA 71360
briansullivan@fs.fed.us

Jon Sweeney
Canadian Forest Service
P.O. Box 4000
Fredericton, NB, Canada E3B 5P7
jsweeney@nrcan.gc.ca

Bob Tatman
Maryland Department of Agriculture
50 Harry S. Truman Pkwy.
Annapolis, MD 21401
nefpm@erols.com

Mark Taylor
Maryland Department of Agriculture
50 Harry S. Truman Pkwy.
Annapolis, MD 21401
taylormc@mda.state.md.us

Ksenia Tcheslavskaia
Dept. Entomology
Virginia Tech
Blacksburg, VA 24061
ktchesla@vt.edu

Harold Thistle
USDA Forest Service
180 Canfield Street
Morgantown,WV 26505
hthistle@fs.fed.us

Kevin Thorpe
USDA, ARS, BARC-West
10300 Baltimore Ave.
Beltsville, MD 20705
Thorpe@ba.ars.usda.gov

Robert Tichenor
Maryland Dept. Agriculture
50 Harry S. Truman Pkwy.
Annapolis, MD 21401
tichenrh@mda.state.md.us

Steve Tilley
Maryland Department of Agriculture
50 Harry S. Truman Pkwy.
Annapolis, MD 21401
tilleys@mda.state.md.us

Patrick Tobin
USDA Forest Service
180 Canfield Street
Morgantown, WV 26505
ptobin@fs.fed.us

Matthew Travis
Maryland Dept. Agriculture
50 Harry S. Truman Pkwy.
Annapolis, MD 21401
travisma@mda.state.md.us

Robert Trumbule
Maryland Dept. Agriculture
6701 Lafayette Ave.
Riverdale, MD 20737
rtrumbule@erols.com

Richard Turcotte
USDA Forest Service
180 Canfield Street
Morgantown, WV 26505
rturcotte@fs.fed.us

Richard Ubbens
City of Toronto -- Forestry
18 Dyas Road, Main Floor
Toronto, Ontario M3B 1V5
rubbens@toronto.ca

James Unger
PA Bureau of Forestry
192 N. Valley Road
Harrisinville, PA 17228
junger@state.pa.us

Algimantas Valaitis
USDA Forest Service
359 Main Road
Delaware, OH 43015
avalaitis@fs.fed.us

Philip van Wassenaer
Ontario Urban Forest Council
544 Exburg Crescent
Mississauga, Ontario L5G 2P4
pwassenaer1022@rogers.com

Robert Venette
USDA Forest Service
1561 Lindig Avenue
St. Paul, MN 55108
rvenette@fs.fed.us

Karen Walker
Prince William County
4092 Merchant Plaza, Ste. A
Woodbridge, VA 22192
kwalker@pwcgov.org

Baode Wang
USDA, APHIS, PPQ
Otis Methods Development Ctr.
Otis ANGB, MA 02542
baode.wang@aphis.usda.gov

Ralph Webb
USDA ARS, Bldg 007, Rm. 301
10300 Baltimore Ave.
Beltsville, MD 20705
webbr@ba.ars.usda.gov

Shahla Werner
PA Bureau of Forestry, DCNR
208 Airport Drive, 2nd Floor
Middletown, PA 17057-5027
shawerner@state.pa.us

Paul Weston
Cornell University
150 Insectary
Ithaca, NY 14853
paw23@cornell.edu

Geoffrey White
USDA ARS, Bldg. 007, Rm. 301
10300 Baltimore Avenue
Beltsville, MD 20705
whiteg@ba.ars.usda.gov

Stefanie Whitmire
University of Puerto Rico
P.O. Box 9030
Mayagüez, PR 00681
Stefanie.Whitmire@mail.wvu.edu

Jacob Wickham
SUNY, CESF, 241 Illick Hall
1 Forestry Drive
Syracuse, NY 13210
jdwickham@syr.edu

Peter Wild
Arborjet, Inc.
70-B Cross St.
Winchester, MA 01890
peterwild@arborjet.com

David Williams
USDA APHIS, PPQ
Bldg. 1398
Otis ANGB, MA 02542
david.w.wlliams@aphis.usda.gov

Tom Wilson
Illinois Dept. Natural Resources
604 E. Franklin
Jerseyville, IL 62052
twilson@dnrmail.state.il.us

Jim Writer
USDA APHIS, PPQ
4700 River Road, Unit 150
Riverdale, MD 20737
jwriter@aphis.usda.gov

Aijun Zhang
USDA ARS, BARC-West
10300 Baltimore Ave.
Beltsville, MD 20705
zhanga@ba.ars.usda.gov

Marion Zuefle
University of Delaware
250 Townsend Hall
Newark, DE 19717
mzuefle@udel.edu

www.ingramcontent.com/pod-product-compliance
Lightning Source LLC
Chambersburg PA
CBHW080303290526
45790CB00005B/1913